The Tanishq Story

Inside India's No. 1 Jewellery Brand

C.K. Venkataraman

 juggernaut

JUGGERNAUT BOOKS
C-I-128, First Floor, Sangam Vihar, Near Holi Chowk,
New Delhi 110080, India

First published by Juggernaut Books 2024

Copyright © C.K. Venkataraman 2024

10 9 8 7 6 5 4 3 2 1

P-ISBN: 9789353455811
E-ISBN: 9789353455552

The views and opinions stated in this book are that of the author's alone and are based on his association with Titan Company Limited and from his various interactions with internal and external stakeholders of Titan. To the best of the author's knowledge, all the facts and figures stated have been verified to the extent possible.

All rights reserved. No part of this publication may be reproduced, transmitted, or stored in a retrieval system in any form or by any means without the written permission of the publisher.

Typeset in Adobe Caslon Pro by R. Ajith Kumar, Noida

Printed at Thomson Press India Ltd

*Dedicated to
Xerxes Desai.
Maverick, visionary, legend, humanitarian,
who threw me out of his office
on a rainy July afternoon in the year 2000
and changed my life forever.*

Contents

Foreword: Why Don't You Become a Well-Known Writer First? … vii

Part 1: The Story

Before the Story (An Indulgent but Short Detour) … 3
1. The Early Days: 1993–2000 … 7
2. When the Going Gets Tough, the Tough Get Going: 2000–2004 … 37
3. On Cruise Control: 2005–2013 … 71
4. The Challenging Years and Recovery: 2013–2019 … 95
5. Leader to Legend: 2019–2023 … 125

Part 2: The Foundations

1. Innovation … 157
2. Customer Obsession … 173
3. Partnership … 191

Contents

4. People — 213
5. Leadership — 225

In Conclusion — 235

Notes — 239
Acknowledgements — 241

Foreword

Why Don't You Become a Well-Known Writer First?

Ever since I was in school, I had always loved writing. But laziness kept my interest in check for many, many years till I started writing in earnest after I turned forty-five. I usually wrote essays – accounts of my childhood in Coimbatore, my bicycle rides in the Bangalore rains or my weekends at my farm. None of these got a double-digit readership, ever, but the appreciation was encouraging. And so I kept at it, writing perhaps an essay a year...

I connected with Chiki Sarkar, the publisher at Juggernaut, when she published the history of the Kohinoor diamond by William Dalrymple and Anita Anand, and reached out to us for a possible sponsorship. That sponsorship did not happen, but I got my foot in the door! Soon after, I gathered the courage to send her one of my essays and she replied – 'you should write a book!'

Around the same time, I had started thinking about work-related stress, which seemed ever present, especially in the corporate world. I had some thoughts on how to manage this and felt that a book on the subject could be useful. I wrote to Chiki with the idea. She liked it, and she gave me a strange piece of advice: *'Why don't you become known as a writer first, before you write that book?'*

'But how do I become known as a writer, without writing my first book?'

'By writing a well-known story first.'

'Which story?'

'The Tanishq story.'

It made total sense, of course, except that I had never thought of writing about Tanishq. I knew much of the story personally, having spent nearly fifteen years in the Jewellery division of Titan Company, from January 2005. I knew some of its earlier history, having heard from others who had been part of the journey between 2000 and 2004, but there were parts – especially during its founding years from 1993 – I didn't know much about.

It was a fascinating story, not only because of its success but also for the formula of its success. The more I thought about Chiki's suggestion, the more I was convinced that it was a story worth telling, particularly for the lessons that it had for people in the corporate world. Tanishq after all had delivered sustained success in excellence, sales growth, profitability and market leadership. What were the philosophies, practices and strategies that had led to this? This book tries to answer this.

Many of the points I have made apply to Titan Company as well, of which Tanishq is a part. But this book is about Tanishq and so I have written my book in the context of the jewellery brand. However, since Tanishq is a brand and Titan is the company and organization behind the brand, I will use the names interchangeably throughout the book depending on the context.

Now back to the philosophies, practices and strategies.

Titan has always been a people-centric company, believing wholly in deep relationships with its employees, through its caring and sharing, often using the word 'family' to describe itself.

Titan has always believed in a multiple-stakeholder focus, in the true Tata way, believing in the right and fair distribution of prosperity to its retail and vendor partners. It has always believed in partnerships forever.

Ethics and integrity have been central to the way Titan works. The name of its corporate campus is *Integrity*.

Tanishq has been devoted to its customers, committed to understanding everything they need and striving to delight them with its products and services.

Tanishq has kept innovation at the centre of its strategy, building differentiation and efficiency through that innovation.

Tanishq is also exceptionally resilient, pulling itself back from the brink of the abyss, when everything seemed lost. It's about the power of self-belief.

Tanishq has been an explorer, charting new territories in redefining the jewellery category, becoming a brand that holds a mirror to its customers' aspirations. It has shaped multiple aspects of the jewellery category and industry through its thought-leadership and influence.

The book explores these through the stories of the many people who were involved in that journey. In part one, I will narrate the chronological story of Tanishq, the early part as a historian, and the latter part as an executive who headed the division as the chief operating officer (COO) between 2005 and 2011, and as the chief executive officer (CEO) between 2012 and 2019. In part two, I will also look at the management lessons Tanishq can teach anyone.

The management lessons are essentially around innovation, customer obsession, the role of leaders and stakeholder focus. I believe that these aspects are fundamental to all businesses and the lessons from one successful business can be applied to other unrelated businesses as well.

Part 1
The Story

Before the Story
(An Indulgent but Short Detour)

Off the coast of Bombay, 6 February 1850, 10 a.m.

Captain Lockyer is quite puzzled, even somewhat worried. He has been to Bombay many times in the last ten years. He has also anchored a few times in these very waters, about a kilometre from the shore. But he has never seen such a choppy sea. The sky has become overcast and rather dark. Streaks of lightning blaze across the sky every two minutes. The waves are over 20 feet tall and unceasing. HMS *Medea*, his strong and reliable vessel, is being buffeted like a little boat from Belfast.

One wouldn't think it is morning. It looks as if the night is setting in.

HMS *Medea* has been contracted by the British East India Company to sail to England and deliver a special package to the palace in London, ultimately meant for the queen herself. The vessel is set to sail today, 6 February. On board are Captain J. Ramsay and Lieutenant Colonel F. Mackeson, in whose care is an iron safe.

Within the safe is a red despatch box, inside which sits a rare gem with a long and chequered history. It was found in a Deccan mine in the twelfth century. Over the next seven centuries, this rare gem changed owners, shape and form, witnessed wars and fratricide, and travelled across a continent, remaining a silent witness to a nation under transformation. The most recent owner was Maharaja Ranjit Singh, the ruler of Punjab.

On 29 March 1849, following the conclusion of the Second Anglo–Sikh War, the Kingdom of Punjab was formally annexed to the East India Company rule. The last Treaty of Lahore was signed and Article III of the treaty read:[1] *'The gem called the Koh-I-Noor, which was taken from Shah Sooja-ool-moolk by Maharajah Ranjeet Singh, shall be surrendered by the Maharajah of Lahore to the Queen of England.'*

This gem, this Koh-I-Noor, this very 'mountain of light' is about to be taken away from its motherland. And it appears that even the heavenly forces are conspiring to keep it from leaving. The winds are screaming, the sea is mad and the rains are pounding the ship.

Some atavistic fear assails Captain Lockyer and he

wants to get away from these shores as fast as possible and head towards his homeland. In an hour, the ship sets sail. The next few hours are gruelling as the vessel comes close to capsizing frequently. It is Lockyer's experience and his resolve that keep the ship afloat. It is only around 6 p.m. that normalcy returns and the crew relaxes.

But even as the ship sails away, the spirit of the Koh-I-Noor leaves its body and escapes the red box, the iron safe and the HMS *Medea* and flees into the ether.

There in the skies, higher than any mortal can reach, the spirit of the Koh-I-Noor floats above Hindustan, biding its time, waiting to be reborn.

One hundred and forty-five years pass.

In 1995, in sleepy Bangalore (now Bengaluru), a visionary is dreaming a daring vision of a new jewel in the Tata group's crown – a stone that will dazzle bright, a gem that will make every woman in this great nation swoon with delight, a diamond that will transform everything in its surroundings. The spirit of the Koh-I-Noor is seized by this extraordinary vision and surges earthward to become one with this daring idea.

Unbeknown to Xerxes Desai, founder and managing director (MD) of Titan Watches, the spirit of the Koh-I-Noor enters his consciousness and is subsumed within the bold, revolutionary idea that is forming in his mind.

C.K. Venkataraman

And, in a flash, the Koh-I-Noor and Tanishq become one.
Is that the true story?
Well, of course not, but it feels good to imagine that it had, in fact, begun like that!

1
The Early Days: 1993–2000

Titan Watches Limited (now Titan Company Limited) was formed in 1984 as a joint venture between the Tata Group and the Tamilnadu Industrial Development Corporation Limited (TIDCO), for manufacturing and selling quartz watches.[2] But the idea for this had been germinating in Tata Press, a printing company that was part of the Tata group, in the 1970s itself, and in the imaginations of Xerxes Desai, the MD of Tata Press, and Anil Manchanda, his deputy.

Xerxes Desai chose to go the 'quartz technology way' for Titan when the whole industry was defined by 'mechanical watches'. The quartz 'movement' was more accurate, had fewer moving parts and cost less to manufacture. For customers, quartz watches were sleeker, more stylish and offered them liberation from having to wind the watch. The visionary in Xerxes Desai saw the watch as an accessory when most of the country saw it as merely a time-keeping device.

Leaders working with HMT, the public-sector watch company, were also convinced about quartz technology. Xerxes's vision attracted some of them and they helped set up a world-class plant in Hosur, Tamil Nadu, which became the foundation of Titan Watches. Titan's product design department, driven directly by Mr Desai, created sleek and elegant styles to match the state-of-the-art manufacturing standards. Full-page newspaper advertisements showcasing dozens of watch models took the brand to the public, tempting them to pick the model of their choice while sipping their morning coffee. A very fresh and elegant TV commercial showcased the range even better, with Mozart's 'Symphony No. 25' providing a Western flavour and imbuing the brand with sophistication and class. A first-of-its-kind exclusive watch showroom added further allure, creating a shopping experience that was international and memorable.

A Symbol of Self-Expression

In just a few years, Titan Watches captured the imagination of the Indian public and became the benchmark in the wristwatch category. While the mechanical-watch-led HMT still had the higher market share in 1990, Titan had run away with the mind share of customers.

The annual report of FY 1989–90 reflects this status:[3]

> Titan is now clearly seen as the most preferred brand in the Indian quartz analogue watch market. Your company has succeeded in displacing the smuggled watches from the price band in which Titan watches are marketed. We have also succeeded in establishing the product as something significantly more than just a time-keeping device – an article to be worn as personal adornment, an expression of the wearer's aesthetic sense and personality.

And, in line with the value system that has remained strong over four decades, the same annual report calls out.

'... The company's employees have been selected with great care and equal care has been taken in their training. They constitute the Company's greatest strength and are a source of pride to all of us.'

Success came very fast to Titan and the business started growing at a brisk clip in the early 1990s. By March 1993, Titan had reached 60 per cent of the share of the quartz analogue market and 12 per cent of the total watch market, an outstanding performance in just six years.

As some of the watches made for the domestic market required imported parts, the import bill started galloping. With the domestic success in the watch category, Xerxes Desai had also developed a global ambition for Titan Watches, centred around a European strategy. After a couple of years of trying to take the Indian product strategy to Europe, it was clear that Titan needed a whole new approach if it were to succeed overseas. The plan was to set up a London office to run operations and marketing, a Paris design office to create the right products and a 'Euro Plant' in Hosur to manufacture these premium watches.

All this needed substantial foreign currency.

In those days, the country was in a precarious situation with respect to its foreign exchange reserves, being able to finance only fifteen days of imports. According to a report in the media in 1991, Reserve Bank of India (RBI) had pledged 47 tonnes of gold to raise around USD 400 million to tide over a balance of payment crisis.[4] It was this compulsion that led to the government encouraging companies to generate foreign exchange to finance their imports. Titan's own accelerating demand for foreign exchange and the government's encouragement around exports were the reasons behind Titan's decision to set up a world-class *jewellery export* manufacturing facility in Hosur.

Catalysing that decision was Mr Desai's visit to a jewellery exhibition in Mumbai sometime in 1990. Mr Desai and Jayanthi Prasad, Titan's public relations head, visited the stalls in that exhibition and the idea of branching into the jewellery business was formed. Given the adjacency of watches and jewellery in European retail stores and some of the common capabilities that watches and jewellery categories needed, it was a natural connection to make. Anil Manchanda, the executive vice president (EVP) of Titan and Mr Desai's right-hand man from the beginning of Titan, was put in charge of the jewellery export project and the concomitant European watch project. The UK-based design and technology firm Grant Walker & Associates (Norman Grant and Mark Walker) was appointed as the project consultant. A pilot workshop was set up inside the watch plant in Hosur and a few jewellery manufacturing experts from the Indian industry were recruited to establish manufacturing processes and techniques. Market-specific product lines based on design advice from Grant Walker and other design consultants were created in that plant.

Anil Manchanda was sceptical about the project from the very beginning and had shared his concerns with Mr Desai, who had brushed them aside. 'Unlike the watch project for which we had researched every aspect at multiple levels, we had jumped into this with very little study of the market,' recalls Anil Manchanda. Nevertheless, a valiant attempt was made to tap into the European jewellery market. 'We met with major buyers in many jewellery centres of Europe with our offerings. We also displayed our wares in 1993 at the INHORGENTA in Munich and during the watch and jewellery fair at Basle, Switzerland. However, there was a huge credibility gap as we had no background in the industry, no manufacturing facility to show and our designs were out of sync with contemporary trends. After a while, it was clear to me that this was not going anywhere and we were chasing a mirage,' says Anil Manchanda.

However, Xerxes Desai was convinced that there was a lucrative opportunity waiting to be tapped and that the venture would ultimately work. Anil Manchanda feels that 'Xerxes was overawed by the glitz and glamour of the luxe watch and jewellery businesses in the fashion centres of Europe'. In mid 1993, Mr Desai decided to take the plans for jewellery and watch exports and for the acquisition of a luxe Swiss watch brand to the Tata Sons board for approval and financial backing. He wanted Anil Manchanda to make the business case and the actual presentation. Anil Manchanda was by then a stronger sceptic of these projects than he had been in the beginning. He refused to present a proposal or to be further involved in projects in which he did not have full confidence and decided to leave Titan. I remember when the news of Anil Manchanda's exit came out; we (I was then a young rookie in the company having joined in 1990) were all quite zapped.

The business case for the jewellery plant was presented to Tata Sons and approved. The unit that was set up in Hosur was the finest kind of plant, coming at an investment of Rs 65 crore – a huge sum in those days. Given Xerxes Desai's general penchant for doing things well, that was not a surprise. However, the strategic rationale for a plant of that nature was not clear. India had a well-developed jewellery industry for export, mostly situated in the Santacruz Electronics Export Processing Zone (SEEPZ), the export promotion zone in Mumbai. Competition was intense, sometimes even cut-throat. Here was a high-end manufacturing unit, without the manufacturing leaders and depth of talent that the watch business had from day one, without business development people who had experience in those international markets. The venture did not seem to make sense. Of course, all this is in hindsight.

Though the focus was on export, particularly the European and American markets, there seemed to have been some plans to launch these in India as well, through a small number of showrooms. A newspaper report of March 1994 refers to this, revealing the brand name to be Celeste, and the emphasis on making 'primarily European jewellery'.

The manufacturing unit began operations sometime in 1994. Weighed down by a higher cost of production, poor knowledge of what American and European jewellers and wholesalers wanted, and a pool of talent that was learning on the job, the export operations sputtered. After months of struggle, it was clear to Xerxes Desai as well that the export opportunity did not quite exist. His focus turned to the domestic jewellery industry, which was huge but totally different from the European and American markets. Everything here was different: the category codes, the types of products that customers bought, the industry structure, the retail practices and the manufacturing methods.

Jewellery in India had existed for centuries, perhaps millennia. It was a store of value and a symbol of wealth.

$30 m Titan unit to make jewellery

BY PRIYA RAMANI

Bombay, March 21: Indian consumers will soon be able to purchase Titan's new jewellery range, Celeste, from a chain of exclusive Titan boutiques across the country.

The Tata-owned, $85 million Titan Industries, that entered the watch business seven years ago, has decided to replicate its succcess in the field of pure gold and gemset jewellery.

A $30 million plant in plant in Bangalore will manufacture 12,000 pieces of finished jewellery every day. Of this 70 per cent will be exported, primarily to Europe and America. The remaining 30 per cent will be sold in the country.

"We will manufacture primarily European jewellery. Even when we use an Indian motif, it will be executed in an international style. Typical Indian jewellery has lots of detailed work but often lacks precision and finish," says Mr Jacob Kurian, general manager, international marketing.

Titan's targetted clientele is the younger crowd who, according to Mr Kurian, are "much more international in their approach."

For the company that sells its designer watches through 4,000 retail outlets across the country, the decision to open exclusive boutiques for its jewellery collection was simple.

"Jewellery is easily copied and once your trust and reputation is damaged it becomes very difficult to earn back consumer confidence. Watches are more difficult to make but with jewellery we're going to be much more careful," he says.

The new collection will be branded and heavily promoted.

The newspaper story mentioning Celeste as the brand name and Titan's plans to 'manufacture primarily European jewellery'

It was also about auspiciousness and purity. Most Indian jewellery was made by hand by *karigar*s (artisans) in small workshops. Indians primarily bought heavily ornamental, intricately designed gold jewellery; gemstones and diamonds were seen as an indulgence. The 22-karat alloy (91.6 per cent pure gold, having 916 parts of gold in a total of 1,000 parts of metal that also included other metals) was the preferred alloy: it was pure enough for the customer and soft enough for the artisan to work on.

Given its value and wealth, jewellery was also *streedhan*, given to the daughter at the time of her wedding. It was also a marker of ethnicity. More than two-thirds of the jewellery made in the early 1990s was wedding jewellery and each state and community had its rituals and trousseau: the Bengali wedding jewellery was different from the Punjabi, which was different from the Telugu and so on. The jewellery was ornate, elaborate and the variety was mind-numbing. This was nothing like what Titan was making for the European market: a small range of 18-karat (750 parts of gold to 1,000 parts of total metal) jewellery, minimal in styling.

Ishaat Hussain served as the Tata Sons' finance director for many years and was on the board of Titan for more than twenty years. He recollects being quite surprised about the decision to enter the domestic jewellery market, especially as a retailer. 'To me, the picture of the Indian jeweller was of the owner sitting on his *gaddi* (cushion), personally overseeing everything in his shop. I just couldn't see how all that could be corporatized.'

Despite all these significant differences, it was decided that Titan would change its direction and enter the domestic market. The circumstances warranted this decision, on account of the huge manufacturing investment that had to be recovered. However, the product-marketing strategy needed to be well-thought-through, given the fact that the plant had been created for the Western markets. Much consumer research needed to be done, to begin with.

Revathi Kant, currently the chief design officer of Titan who oversaw Titan Company's market research then, remembers suggesting carrying out market research to see how receptive people would be to buying 18-karat jewellery instead of 22-karat. But no research was conducted and Titan plunged into making 18-karat jewellery for the Indian consumer. Xerxes was confident that Titan would transform the jewellery market just as it had transformed the watch market.

The strategy was multifold: The brand would offer more diamond jewellery than gold. Gold jewellery prices were transparent and everyone was making the same kind of product. Diamond jewellery could be differentiated and would be more profitable. The stores would be fashioned after European boutiques and position the brand as an exquisite jewellery store. The staff would be carefully chosen for their sophistication.

David Saldanha was the head of retailing in the Watch division and was appointed as the head of the domestic jewellery project some time in 1994. He remembers being told by Xerxes Desai that he needed to set up twenty stores in two years. That remit took him to London, Paris, Milan and a few other European cities on a recce trip. Xerxes Desai was closely involved in the store design, wanting to create 'the Tiffany of the East'. David signed up four company-owned and fourteen franchisee store locations, thereafter, paving the way for the speedy launch of Tanishq in various cities.

Another newspaper article in 1994 quotes: 'The company is getting the well-known Austrian designer Hans Hollein to design these exclusive, upmarket jewellery shops.'

But ultimately, the assignment went to an Indian architect and designer, Kiran Patki.

It's also not clear how the name Celeste got dropped. Obviously, between the time when Celeste had been finalized (mid 1994) and when the first Tanishq store opened (mid 1996), enough time had passed for a reconsideration. The story of how the name Tanishq was finalized is fascinating. Meera Harish, a veteran at Titan, remembers poring over books at the suggestion of Xerxes Desai to come up with the ideal name. One of the names she had circled from a book was Nishka, which meant a 'throat ornament'. Xerxes played with it, knocking off the 'a' and replacing the 'k' with a 'q', converting it to Nishq. He felt it sounded more exotic. Then, in a flash of inspiration, he added a 'ta' in the front, creating Tanishq. Over time, the name came to be interpreted in different ways: representing Tata and Tamil Nadu in one interpretation and combining 'tan' (body) and 'ishq' (love) in another.

The first up-market Tanishq store opened in Cathedral Road, Chennai in July 1996. As planned, it was a boutique fashioned after the finest stores of the European capitals, where customers were supposed to fix an appointment with the store manager before their visit! The jewellery was all 18-karat diamond jewellery, very Western in its appeal. The sales staff were like 'air hostesses', as a colleague of that time recalls.

Latha Padmanabhan, the store manager at that time, who ultimately retired as the regional business manager of Tanishq in 2016, recalls, 'The walk-in was quite low most

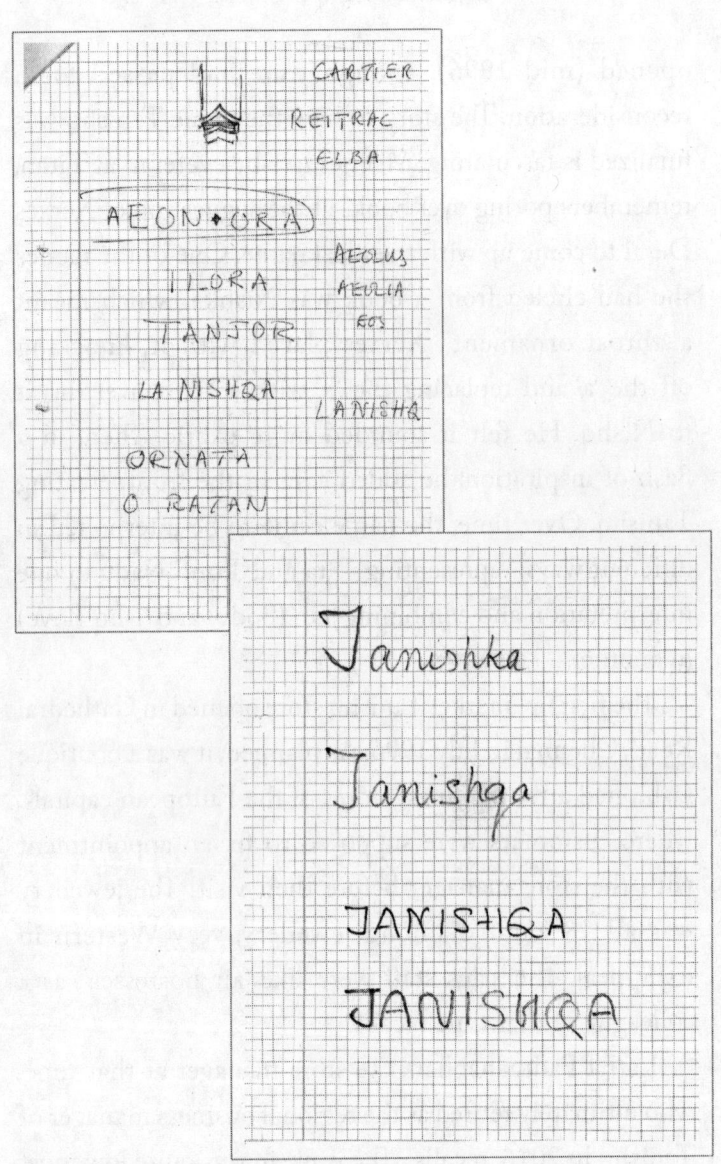

Xerxes Desai's doodles on the way to coining one of India's most iconic brand names

The Tanishq launch ad campaign, sometime in 1995, pre-dating the first store launch in 1996. The jewellery was sold at that time through other jewellers and Titan Watch showrooms.

of the first year. The feedback was very clear; we needed 22-karat jewellery.'

David Saldanha and the team responded quickly. They went to Mumbai and Mysore, contacted jewellery manufacturers and got some 22-karat jewellery made. This improved the walk-in situation significantly, but the bulk of the product lines were still 18-karat diamond jewellery, misaligned both on the store-of-value and design needs of the customers. The Chennai store struggled in its first year, closing at Rs 2.8 crore of sales against a target of Rs 3.5 crore.

Of course, the introduction of the 22-karat jewellery, however small at that time, was a crucial change in the direction. 'To give Mr Desai credit, he realized that this was badly needed, even if it did not fit his vision,' David is graceful in his recollection. Then mirth takes over. 'We, first of all, got it wrong in terms of what the Western people liked. And then we assumed that what they didn't like, the Indian people would like!'

Titan's 1996–97 Annual Report calls for attention to the growing importance of 22-karat jewellery:[5]

While the company believes that an 18-karat gold alloy is the most-suited for jewellery – and is, in fact, the world standard for fine gold jewellery – the existence of a very strong consumer preference in India for 22-karat gold jewellery cannot be wished away. Our entry into this market segment will, it is hoped, accelerate the trend towards an official hallmarking process which will significantly benefit the consumer who, today, is often the recipient of substantially undercarataged jewellery masquerading under the 22-karat label.

This acknowledgement, written in the style that evokes Xerxes, does not seem to go all the way through and appears more like a grudging acceptance of a challenging situation rather than an enthusiastic embrace of a new, exciting path.

Sometime in 1997, around the time this annual report came out, Vasant Nangia, who had been the head of Titan's international business based in London, was moved to head the jewellery business and David Saldanha went to London in his place. Vasant created a larger team by bringing in a few more Titan veterans. More traditional 22-karat gold jewellery was created and launched with considerable ad support, and standard industry practices like showing the gold weight, diamond quality and weight and making charges separately were also started in his time. Quarterly buying meets were started, where the company teams presented the new product lines to the

Fashioned after the luxury stores of Europe, the early Tanishq 'boutiques' were quite elitist and forbidding.

franchisees and staff for systematic ordering as well as for building ownership. All these helped, but the big differentiator was still missing.

M.S. Shantharam was the head of manufacturing for jewellery from 1994 and retired as the chief manufacturing officer of Watches in the early 2000s. On a visit to the Basel Jewellery and Watch Show in 1996, he had seen an X-ray fluorescence machine that could determine the elements in a metal alloy in a very short time, without damaging it. Vasant and the team immediately saw the potential in this machine.

The single biggest benefit from gold jewellery was (and still is) its 'store of value'. Because of this, the public had been wary of paying high making charges[6] for decades, so, when they needed to convert the jewellery into cash, very little was lost. This put considerable pressure on the industry with respect to profitability and even viability. Over time, many jewellers ended up selling lower karat alloys in place of 22-karat, to make profit. So, customers ended up paying the low making charges which they wanted, but also ended up getting 19-karat or 20-karat jewellery (or even lower karatage) in the place of the 22-karat jewellery that they thought they were buying. Underkaratage was rampant in the industry. Tests of jewellery from across the country had clearly established this fact to the people within Titan. But the way to demonstrate this to the customers remained elusive since it meant destroying the jewellery by melting it for testing. That was obviously not feasible.

The X-ray fluorescence machine provided a fabulous solution to that problem. Through a non-destructive process, it could break up the gold alloy into its constituent elements: gold, silver, copper, whatever – in just three minutes!

This machine was called XRF, an X-ray fluorescence Spectrometer. It had been originally designed to assess combinations of all 100+ periodic elements. Titan had first bought it for its lab, for broad-spectrum alloy testing. The gold alloy standards that the XRF was designed for were only 75 per cent (18 karat) and 91.6 per cent (22 karat). India sold multiple karat types and the XRF needed to be able to measure those accurately. Alagappan, head of Tanishq's Customer Service today, recollects starting with forty-five to fifty types of gold alloys, sitting with the programming people of the manufacturer of the XRF and reprogramming the machine for Titan's specific requirements. This machine was to become a game-changer for Tanishq ultimately.

In 1997, Vasant Nangia and team had the machine deployed in multiple boutiques nationwide. Each machine cost more than Rs 10 lakh and it must have taken a lot of conviction and guts for such an investment, given the financial state of Tanishq at that time. But the team had the conviction and guts and ended up creating the most critical differentiation that Tanishq was desperately waiting for. This gave Tanishq a little more time to breathe.

The Karatmeter, as branded by the Lintas team and the then head of the Tanishq account, Joseph George (Joe, who went on to become group chairman of Lowe Lintas in 2016), ended up becoming the bedrock of Tanishq's value proposition, a powerful symbol of purity. Stories are legion about the Karatmeter's use at that time. Hundreds of people standing in queue for testing, customers breaking down after discovering the actual purity of their jewellery and then becoming irate about the jeweller who had gypped them, the local jewellery industry leaning heavily on the Tanishq franchisees to desist from using it, some jewellers even threatening violent action.

The Karatmeter changed the brand's marketing approach. The filmmaker R. Balki was the creative director of Lintas Bangalore from the mid to late 1990s and was very closely involved with Tanishq along with Joe (Balki went on to become group chairman of Lowe Lintas around 2007).

BEWARE, THERE'S A THIEF IN THE FAMILY.

In Mrs Meena Agarwal's eyes, her jeweller was not an outsider. She trusted him no less than she trusted her family members. All this changed on 30th July, 1998. The day we invited Mrs Agarwal to our showroom and offered to test the 22 karat necklace that she had bought from her jeweller.

It was a simple procedure. The necklace was placed on a computerised karatmeter (the same machine that is used to test the purity of gold, the world over) and, in 180 seconds, we had the result. Mrs Agarwal's necklace was actually made of 18.3 karat gold. She was embarassed and her trust in the jeweller was shattered.

This is a true story of a woman who bought gold jewellery without knowing its exact karatage.

But when you buy jewellery from Tanishq, you can be sure. The gold used is painstakingly refined, alloyed and verified for its exact karatage. This stringent quality control process is carried out at our jewellery manufacturing facilities. So, when you buy 22 karat jewellery, you get jewellery that is precisely 22 karat.

That's not all, every piece of Tanishq jewellery comes with a guarantee. A guarantee that gives women like Mrs Agarwal a reason to place their trust in Tanishq.

If you too want to get your jewellery tested*, we will do it for you, free of cost, at the Tanishq showroom.

TANISHQ
PRECIOUS JEWELLERY
GUARANTEED BY TITAN

*Testing facilities available at the showroom only for a limited period. The Tanishq Showroom: City Centre, M.G. Road, Indore. (0731) 540379.

Pulling absolutely no punches! One of the early, and perhaps the most effective, Karatmeter ads.

'Xerxes was always reluctant about 22-karat Indian jewellery,' recalls Balki. In Balki's vivid recollection, Xerxes did not want to make Tanishq *'yet another Indian jewellery brand'*. Balki remembers being in this complex situation, where 22-karat jewellery was where the business was, but the founder MD was dead against the brand proposition built on that! Balki remembers being stuck and desperately looking for an angle.

'The Karatmeter gave us the angle that we were desperately looking for, with which we could build a story for Tanishq that Xerxes was comfortable with,' Balki recollects. Joe adds, 'Suddenly, the purity story became the anchor and Xerxes was sold!' Vinod Moolacherry, copy trainee at Lintas, wrote, in Balki's words, 'What was perhaps the most powerful headline of his life: "Beware, there's a thief in your family!" It was a direct reference to the family jewellers and their unfair practices,' Balki pauses in recollection. 'That one ad, and what followed from that, changed the fate of Tanishq forever. The Tiffany of the East, which was Xerxes Desai's vision for Tanishq, had moved on to a different course altogether. Even though we did not know it then.'

(I could see that the 'Tiffany of the East' dream never went away for Mr Desai. Even though he was quite proud of what Tanishq had achieved, he was perhaps not that fond of

what Tanishq had become. On a visit to a Bengaluru Tanishq store with me around 2010, he was a bit taken aback by the jewellery he saw on one of the counters. He said, 'My god, Venkat! Who buys all these?' I could also play his game. I smiled and said, 'Not Europeans, Mr Desai!' And when he visited the Mumbai Zoya [Titan's luxury jewellery brand] store around 2011 at my request, he wrote me a one-line mail: This is the Tanishq that I had always wanted!)

When Balki and team presented the purity story underpinned by the Karatmeter, he accepted it because 22-karat was where the game was and the idea of transparency and trust gave Tanishq the license to play that game. Mr Desai's insistence on a unique story for Tanishq and his stubbornness in not getting railroaded into making it yet another 22-karat-jewellery brand was how Tanishq came to have such a differentiated brand value proposition.

Starting in 1997, the Karatmeter exposed the bad practices prevalent in the industry and provided a key differentiator to Tanishq that had the potential to change its trajectory substantially. But a few things were still in the way. The product line had still not transformed fully into the relevant Indian 22-karat jewellery that the market needed. The stores were still the 'Western' boutiques which were somewhat intimidating, with staff who were 'distant and formal'.

These remained unaddressed, perhaps because of the original dream that persisted as a hope. Maybe Xerxes saw the entire 22-karat journey more as a detour through which Tanishq would rejoin the path that he had envisioned, to an end that the rest of the world had already reached. Given his upbringing, his aesthetic standards and his Oxford education, that was the worthy goal.

It was natural that a visionary would see things that other normal people couldn't. The strategy behind Titan Watches and its quick success was proof of that. However, much of the rest of the world had gone from chunky mechanical watches to sleek quartz watches, particularly in the volume market, driven by the Japanese companies. There was a global precedent for that and there was no reason why it would not have happened in India. Xerxes Desai's vision and strategy substantially accelerated it and advanced it by many years.

But the jewellery category was very different. In India, jewellery was a store of value. It was an investment, often vying with real estate and the stock markets for a share of the wallet. It was a cultural identity that differentiated a Bengali bride from a Gujarati one. In America or Europe, jewellery was none of these.

The diamond jewellery focus of Tanishq went against this need. The styling of the products did not help either.

And the stores were 'boutiques'. Visualized from the best localities of Europe, they looked like art galleries inside with padded walls, paintings and marble facades that evoked the look and mood of high-end restaurants. In Mumbai's Churchgate store, for instance, Vilas Shinde, an artist friend of the franchisee Ajeet Arenja, hand-painted the 200 square feet ceiling, lying down on his back on a scaffolding for four weeks because Xerxes Desai wanted it done that way (evoking to me the commissioning of the Sistine Chapel ceiling painting by Michelangelo at the insistence of the Pope).

When a vision runs quite counter to the dynamics of the marketplace, how does an organization alter its direction, how does it course-correct?

It's quite axiomatic that in visionary-led organizations, the influence of the visionary is so great that everyone believes them, or perhaps no one dares to question him or her. Anil Manchanda was the only person who had a strong influence on Xerxes Desai, but even he could not prevail over him.

How much did Xerxes Desai attempt to align his leadership team to his vision? Was it his style that kept the others out? Or did his deep belief in his vision, which was not shared by others, become a barrier and made him dig his heels in?

What are the lessons here? As leaders, how comfortable are we about having strong personalities around us who offer counterpoints – people who push us hard, who force us to blink? How do we learn to distinguish our conviction from our hubris? Was it a deep conviction that made Xerxes Desai ignore Anil Manchanda's point or Revathi's suggestion, or was it his hubris? Was it belief or arrogance? We will never know, of course, especially since Xerxes Desai is not here to present his view, but it would be good to question ourselves when we encounter a similar situation in our lives.

At the same time, the passion that Xerxes Desai had for anything he took on and the obsession that he put into every detail was inspirational. Everyone who worked with him was touched by all that gold dust and came away better for it.

The naming of Tanishq was certainly genius at work. The differentiated strategy that would evolve over time to make Tanishq jewellery an accessory, an object of grace and beauty, an expression of special relationships and a symbol of refinement and discernment had started with a name which had many of these dimensions already synthesized in its sound and, soon, in its visual form as well. It was only a man like Xerxes Desai who could create an exotic name like that, looking into the distant future while he did that.

C.K. Venkataraman

Whenever I think of Xerxes Desai and his visioning ability, I recall a powerful line from the Lawrence of Arabia:[7]

> All men dream, but not equally. Those who dream by night in the dusty recesses of their mind wake in the morning to find it is vanity; but the dreamers of the day are dangerous men, for they act their dreams with open eyes to make it possible.

But this dream, as it turned out, had to wait for some years to become a reality. From 1996 to 2000, it was a continuous struggle for Titan Company. The misadventure in the European watch market was sucking a lot of funds. The international watch operations in West Asia, headquartered in Dubai, were a consistent success from day one, but that was not enough to compensate for the European losses. The domestic jewellery business was also losing money and aggravating the overall company situation.

Debt was high and the cash flows were very meagre. S. Rajarathnam, a Titan Finance department veteran who had seen these tough times, recollects that the financial IT system would automatically print all the supplier cheques a few days ahead of the due date (as it had been programmed to do) and the pile of cheques would build on his desk. His team would pull out all the cheques below Rs 5,000 for him to sign as Titan was very particular about payments to small firms. The rest would wait as Raj and the team did a lot of juggling of the current cashflows and desperately imagined what the next few days would bring.

From an 8.9 per cent profit margin in FY 1995 and a Rs 554 crore market cap in May 1995, Titan Company crashed to a 3.4 per cent profit margin in FY 2000 and a Rs 311 crore market cap in May 2000.

Things were looking bad.

2

When the Going Gets Tough, the Tough Get Going: 2000–2004

As we had seen in the last chapter, Tanishq was launched in India in 1996 with a vision to make it the 'Tiffany of the East'. That dream defined the early strategy: European-style 18-karat diamond jewellery, marble-encased boutiques that were a bit forbidding, air hostess-style sales staff and elitist advertising. Despite the introduction of 22-karat gold jewellery in 1997 and the introduction of the Karatmeter soon thereafter, the business continued to struggle which began to affect Titan Industries (the name had changed after the company had entered the jewellery business) significantly. The company was already under pressure from its losses in Europe, owing to the failed watch operations and was winding up the business there.

Many people within Titan, members of the Titan board and several leaders from Tata, including some directors of Tata Sons were wondering why Titan was in an industry where no corporation was ever likely to succeed.

To compound its troubles, Tanishq had its Y2K shock. In May of 2000, Vasant Nangia, who had been the business head of Tanishq since 1997, suddenly left Titan to create a jewellery start-up. Many of his senior colleagues left with him. Things couldn't have been more challenging for Tanishq and Titan. Xerxes Desai must have had his back totally to the wall. Had I been him, I may have looked up to the heavens in frustration and asked, 'God, seriously?'

Spiritualists say that everything happens for a reason. Jacob Kurian had joined Titan in 1993 as general manager, International Marketing, reporting to Anil Manchanda (who left Titan a few months later). Between 1993 and 1996, he was part of the international business leadership team, along with Vasant Nangia who headed the European operations from London, and S. Ravi Kant, who headed the Middle East Operations from Dubai. All these leaders reported to Xerxes Desai.

I was in the domestic Watches business as the marketing manager and had no interaction with Jacob. But his reputation was that of a very tough and demanding boss. So, I was jolted when Bhaskar Bhat, my boss and SVP of

Sales and Marketing in 1997, told me that Xerxes Desai was bringing Jacob into the domestic division as VP of Marketing. This meant that I would report to him. I can still remember the extreme unease that I felt as soon as I heard this. We were in Kochi at a watch dealer meet when Bhaskar had chosen to tell me this, and as soon as I heard the news, I tuned out of the event, unable to think of anything else. I could barely sleep that night, so high was my anxiety.

Jacob – or at least what I had heard about him – was not the boss I wanted. My gut told me that we were so unlike each other that it just wouldn't work. I ran through some imaginary conversations with Mr Desai where I ended up getting transferred to another department or, worse, leaving Titan.

Thankfully, through those tosses and turns in bed, better sense prevailed. By the time I was back in Bengaluru, I had not only reconciled to this new development but was starting to look forward to it as well. On the following Monday, I went to Mr Desai and thanked him for bringing Jacob to head the Marketing and how all of us and the company were going to benefit from it. I could see that he was quite happy and relieved.

Thus began a three-year journey with Jacob that would leave a big impact on me.

We often confuse, at work and home, surface-level characteristics of people as determinants of compatibility and end up placing too much value on them. This approach often leads to conflict. For instance, most arguments at home happen over the unwashed dishes, the uncleared garbage, the lights that were left on or the water bill that was not paid on time, creating tensions between a couple who were otherwise deeply connected through their shared values of fairness, compassion, transparency and ethics. How easy it would be if either of the couple simply adjusted a little and worked together to resolve these conflicts! And so is it at work. The ultra-tough guy, Jacob, as he appeared to be from a distance, seemed very different up close. I started appreciating the many things that he really was defined by and how much they meant to me as well: simplicity in thinking, focus and effectively prioritizing workload, his value of time and punctuality and work-life balance. He also possessed qualities that I was not aware I lacked, but came to realize that I needed: frankness, even bluntness, a strong bias for action and an intolerance for bullshit.

Over the next three years, we worked very effectively together. I learnt a lot from him and continued to apply some of those things well into the future. An organizational restructuring around March 2000 made him the chief strategy officer (CSO) of the whole company, reporting to Mr Desai. It was bittersweet news for me that time; bitter as I had eventually grown to respect him and sweet because I was going to be the boss of Watches, Marketing, reporting to Bijou Kurien, who was now VP of Sales and Marketing of Watches, who reported to Bhaskar Bhat, COO, Watches.

When Vasant Nangia left Titan in May 2000, Xerxes Desai turned to Jacob to take over Tanishq. Jacob recollects not being keen about it, but feeling obligated to take up the job because the company needed that intervention and Mr Desai was personally requesting him. But he insisted on two things: one, the manufacturing would also report to him (between 1996 and 2000, the manufacturing arm of Tanishq had directly reported to Mr Desai and not to David Saldanha or Vasant Nangia); and two, Mr Desai would give total freedom to Jacob and not interfere. Mr Desai agreed to these and Jacob became the COO of Tanishq (technically of the Jewellery division) in May 2000.

The next two years would alter the destiny of Tanishq forever.

As a result of many people leaving with Vasant, the sales and marketing team had to be built afresh. V. Govind Raj, a Titan veteran who was heading Watches sales for the West region in Mumbai, was pulled in to head Retail for Tanishq; Y.L. Saroja, who had spent six years in Watches sales and marketing, came back to the company after a six-month break to head Marketing; Antony Motha, having spent nearly ten years with Titan Finance, including in Jewellery factory finance, was roped in to head Commercial; many others joined over the next year.

Close up, the challenges seemed insurmountable.

Most of the stores continued to look like European 'boutiques' and came across as luxurious and intimidating. While the product lines had improved over the years, the absence of an integrated go-to-market strategy had kept the relevance low. The customer value proposition had still not formed and the price perception was negative. *Not enough people were walking into the stores.*

On one of his early visits to Hyderabad, Jacob remembers witnessing a customer screaming his head off in the store about a finger ring that he had ordered for a family wedding that had not been delivered on time. Worse, no one knew where it was! It was a terrible situation with the salesperson having to take the brunt of the customer's anger. Because of the batch production that the factory followed, alignment with customer and store requirements was unpredictable. *Operations were inefficient.*

Saroja remembers attending her first Business Associate Meet (BAM, an annual meeting with the franchisee partners) in June of 2000 and being scared to meet all of them together, and being swamped by a flood of emotions and shortcomings. She remembers meeting them one at a time and how her notebook was overflowing with their complaints. *The partners were sceptical.*

In a board meeting soon after he moved in, Jacob recollects Ishaat Hussain telling him that the Tata Group was veering towards closing the jewellery business. He also remembers one of the TIDCO directors who was with them, remarking that the jewellery market in Panagal Park, Chennai, was quite large – implying that this was a large opportunity, and the team should be given time. Ishaat Hussain, the gentleman he was, then whispered to Jacob that the decision had already been taken, but he had twelve months. *The pressure from the top was high.*

Over the next two years, the team found innovative solutions to many of these challenges.

Not Enough People Were Walking into the Stores

On a visit to a Bengaluru store, Jacob met an irate customer when she was storming out of the store after learning that the '22-karat' jewellery that she had purchased from somewhere else was only 17-karat. The Karatmeter was well known by then and was in extensive use across all stores. She told Jacob that Tanishq seemed to derive joy from making customers feel terrible but offered no solution to that problem. Jacob was so shaken by that episode that he went back to the office and put everyone on a job to solve the customer's problem. The result of that huddle was the transformational 'Impure-to-Pure' programme that subsequently became the '19 = 22' programme.

This is how the 19 = 22 was designed to work. Let's say, a customer brought in gold jewellery purchased from elsewhere which turned out to be 16-karat, which was 666 parts of purity (16/24×1,000) per 1,000. The Tanishq gold jewellery itself was 22-karat, which was 916 parts of purity (22/24×1,000) per 1,000. In this example, the customer would pay the difference between 666 parts and 791 parts (19/24×1,000) and Tanishq would pick up the difference between 791 parts and 916 parts (while this may sound quite complicated to the lay reader, particularly men, it was quite simple for women who were used to buying jewellery). Basically, the customer would pick up the difference between the actual karat and 19 karat and Tanishq would give them 22-karat jewellery in its place. This was done only when the customer purchased

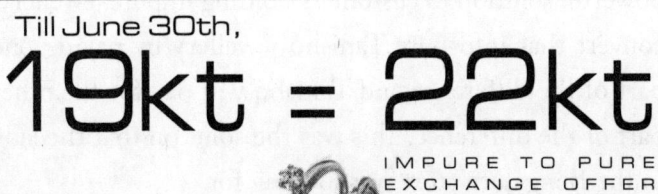

The 19 = 22 gold exchange ad for the programme that created a whole new stream of customer acquisition and revenue

Tanishq's jewellery worth at least the value of the gold that she was giving in.

Through this programme, Tanishq provided a very powerful solution to customers holding impure jewellery: convert that into pure Tanishq jewellery by paying one part of the difference and Tanishq will pay for the other part of the difference. This was the solution that the lady in the Bengaluru store was looking for.

Jacob remembers that the chief financial officer (CFO) of Titan Watches, Khushroo Kapadia, was aghast when this idea was proposed to him. Kapadia was not clear about the economics of the scheme. Tanishq was giving 3 karats (22-19) free to the customer. That was the equivalent of giving '12 per cent off' (3/24×100%), in a category where the margin was already very low. But Jacob was betting on customers buying substantially more jewellery than they were exchanging (100 per cent or more) and, thereby, bringing down the cost of sales to under 6 per cent. After much discussion, Jacob's view prevailed.

The 'Impure to Pure' programme was launched with substantial success. It combined an industry situation (low purity given by many jewellers), an innovative machine (the Karatmeter which could determine the exact purity without damaging the jewellery) and a customer problem ('now what do I do?') into a win-win for both the customer

The Tanishq Story

and Tanishq, and ultimately converted the sceptics to loyalists. Today, the General Exchange Programme (as it has been called for more than fifteen years now) has become a new-customer acquisition route as well as a mode of payment for repeat customers and contributes to about 30 per cent of the sales of Tanishq.

Where is the place for the leader? To use the military analogy, is it in the command HQ or is it in the trenches? While the answer will vary with the type of industry and the type of situation, one thing is clear – every leader should spend adequate time in the trenches, so that they are in touch with reality all the time and alive to every opportunity for creating value. Now imagine Jacob sitting in his office and the feedback about that Karatmeter customer experience, secondhand. He may have nodded his head, empathized with that customer's situation and gone about his life. But because he made the effort to be on the floor of the store where the action happens, he got it from her squarely between his eyes. It shook him, disturbed him no end and Impure to Pure was born. *So, yes, do spend time in the trenches and put yourself in the line of fire.*

Extensive research conducted in the early part of 2001 indicated that the biggest barrier to customers walking into Tanishq was the perception of price. 'The perception was six to seven times the reality!' Jacob chuckles. While Tanishq was more expensive than other jewellery brands, the stores, the staff and the advertising had combined to give it a luxury image which was not true. The price premium had to be maintained, but, at the same time, many more customers had to be drawn into the store.

The jewellery industry was not used to making any discount offers to customers on account of the low margins in the category. But Saroja had worked in the Watches division of Titan and was used to consumer promotions. She went to Jacob with the basic idea. It helped that Tanishq had recently done a 'private' discount sale in Hosur, managed by the employees of the factory, which had done very well. Jacob encouraged Saroja to do it and told her, 'Let's go *big* or go *home*!'

The initial campaign proposal was the '5th Anniversary Sale. Up to 5% off'. Saroja remembers Jacob laughing them out of the room, saying, '*Guys, didn't I tell you to go big or go home?*' The final promotion was called 'The Freedom Sale, up to 20% off!' and was timed to end at midnight on 14 August 2001, just in time to welcome Independence Day. After a couple of days of low response, the scheme just took off and became the biggest blockbuster in the five years of Tanishq. Saroja recollects with tears in her eyes, 'At 1 a.m. on 15 August, a couple of us were in the Dickenson Road, Bengaluru store. Raja Uppalapatti (our Vizag franchisee) called me and said, after today Tanishq will never look back!'

The sceptics were turning around.

Even today, consumer promotions of various types are interwoven with brand campaigns and collection launches to deliver great customer delight and sales growth throughout the year.

Operations Were Quite Inefficient

You may recollect that the Tanishq factory was set up for the international market and was hoping to sell to networks of jewellery stores. The idea was to create a reasonable number of 18-karat diamond jewellery items, make multiple pieces of each and sell them through many stores. The technology and process were set up for that. The technology used was 'casting' and the manufacturing process was 'batch'.

Cast jewellery was made in the following way. For example, after a ring was designed, a silver master (replica) was made by hand by a skilled craftsperson. Thereafter, a negative of this silver was cut into a rubber mould. Then, wax was injected into the rubber mould to get a wax replica of the ring. Based on the sales team's requirements, multiple wax pieces (of rings, pendants, earrings), made in a similar manner, would then be fused onto a thin wax cylinder to result in what is called a 'wax tree'. This wax tree would then be encased in gypsum powder and baked, leaving within that powder mould, the negative of that wax tree (the wax would have melted through the baking). Molten 18-karat gold would then be injected into the gypsum mould and cooled. The gold would occupy the space left by the wax and form an identical shape. The powder mould would then be broken to create an 18-karat gold tree. The gold 'pieces' would be filed off the gold trunk for artisans who would then refine the objects, fix the diamonds and polish them to create the final products.

The issue was in the manual processes that followed: bench working, diamond setting and polishing. These were done by different sets of people because they needed different skills. Let's take the ring we have been talking about. Given its size, the bench working (refining the form and shape of that ring with hand tools and giving it strong definitions) would be finished in a few hours. But if all the diamond setters had been loaded with complex products over the last couple of days, they would still be setting diamonds on necklaces, bangles and pendants.

The Tanishq Story

This ring would lie waiting, till any one diamond setter was free to take it on. This was the cause of the delay in the delivery of the wedding ring in Hyderabad and the customer screaming his head off.

Tanishq needed a single-piece flow. There were three different departments – bench working, stone setting and polishing – within which the product flow was stuck. Somaiya, an expert consultant in world-class manufacturing, was hired sometime in 2000. The 'single-cell' idea was brought in by him and the Tanishq manufacturing team, where a team of bench workers, setters and polishers would sit together and complete each product in a sequence. Their original proposal to Jacob was that it would take three to four months to modify the layout to accommodate the single-cell process. Palani Kumar, senior VP, Integrated Retail Services, Titan Company, who was part of the Tanishq manufacturing team in 2000, smiles in recollection, 'Jacob threw us out of the room with a laugh!' With Somaiya's help, the new layout for the 'cell' concept was completed within five days during Diwali.

After a few years, the 'single-cell' process became a 'single-person cell,' where each employee learnt all three skills (bench working, stone setting and polishing) and became capable of completing the entire 'downstream' operation by themselves. This enabled uninterrupted product flow, maximized productivity and transformed employee ownership and morale.

One quality of transformational leaders is their ability to set 'big hairy audacious goals' and get their teams to believe that they are achievable. The initial assessment was that the factory layout change would take three to four months. To Jacob's impatient mind, this kind of thinking would have been absolutely unacceptable. *Things are burning all around us, and you guys are taking your own sweet time?* Laughing them out of the room was his way of saying the same thing. Only such leaders can make people stretch inside a pressure cooker. Very few leaders would have the audacity *even to think of such an 'impossible' target*, let alone ask for it. But Jacob did succeed.

Much of the diamond jewellery of Tanishq was made in the sophisticated plant that had been set up in 1994 and the cost of production was high. However, most of the 22-karat gold jewellery was (and continues to be) outsourced from vendors. There was a need for cost reduction here as well. One of the characteristics of this industry was the aggregator-trader who liaised with multiple head-*karigar*s, each of whom had fifty or hundred bench-*karigar*s (the artisans who made the jewellery) working under them in small workshops. This was how it worked in Kolkata and most other locations. The vendors would typically charge their conversion charges as a per cent of the price of gold. Jacob wanted an alternate model of production, which shaved off a per cent or two from the labour charges which would flow directly to the bottom line. He gave this remit to Sukumaran, currently the general manager of the Supply Chain for the Jewellery division. Sukumaran went to Mumbai and met Kamlesh Vyas, a jewellery manufacturer who was selling his jewellery all over India to independent jewellers. Kamlesh and his brother Rajesh were looking for professionalism, safety and business security. They signed up with Tanishq and became the founders of the first 'karigar park'. The karigar park was a small unit with fifty to hundred *karigar*s, under the direct supervision of the owner, who was also a jewellery manufacturing expert. The karigar park came with two advantages for Tanishq: one was the ability to deal directly with the owner/head *karigar* and the other was the opportunity to get *karigar*s to work for a monthly pay as opposed to weight-output-based pay determined as a per cent of the price of gold. Both helped Tanishq to bring its costs down and the monthly pay approach protected *karigar*s during the lean months. Karigar parks (and their evolved version, Karigar Centres) became an important part of the sourcing strategy.

'We had two young children. And we were Gujaratis who had always lived in Mumbai. But we just took a leap of faith. It took me three weeks longer than what Sukumaran gave, but we relocated our entire operation to Hosur with two trucks full of equipment and tools and a hundred *karigar*s to set up the first karigar park of Tanishq,' Kamlesh recalls with pride.

As I listen to Kamlesh and Rajesh, I marvel at the entrepreneurial nation that we are. How many millions of people have uprooted themselves and their families and moved thousands of kilometres to start a whole new life, full of uncertainties and risks? In search of a better life, a brighter future and, almost always, a burning dream propelling them forward.

The 'single-cell' manufacturing of diamond jewellery and the karigar park were two transformative innovations. The diamond grade change was another decision with a significant long-term impact.

Like the 18, 22 and 24 karat purity definition for gold, diamonds had their own classification method: the 4 Cs – clarity, cut, colour and carat (factors that define a diamond's value). The first three aspects were about quality dimensions of the diamonds and the fourth was about their weight. Clarity defined the extent of 'inclusions' inside a diamond: from FL, which was flawless, to VVS, which had very, very small inclusions, to VS, which had very small inclusions and so on. Cut (a human's contribution to a diamond) had its own ranges dispersed around the excellent cut, which had fifty-seven facets on the round brilliant diamond. The best colour started with D and went down to K, L, M. A single carat had 100 cents, so you could have a 5-cent diamond, 10-cent diamond, etc. and, of course, 2 carat, 5 carat and so on.

Because of some historical reasons, the 'inclusions' were considered 'impurities', particularly in South India, that brought bad luck to the wearer. So, the popular clarity in Tamil Nadu, Telangana and Andhra was VVS, a very expensive grade of diamond. Because of this, diamond jewellery has remained targeted at the well-to-do and the wealthy class. The fact that clarity also defines the rarity of a diamond (meaning VVS diamonds occur far less on the earth when compared to SI diamonds) and does not have a 'deal-breaker' role in the brilliance and scintillation (cut delivers that more) was not appreciated by the Tanishq team that much.

Bharat Jhaveri was a jewellery industry veteran who had come into Tanishq sometime in 2001 and had become category manager for diamond necklaces, bangles and earrings in 2004. Bharat recalls fondly, 'The good thing about Tanishq was that you could pitch your idea to the leaders irrespective of your position. They would listen.' Till then Tanishq was using the very-high quality diamonds, VVS in GH colour. Some of the big jewellers were using VS diamonds in GH colour (the term was Super Deluxe). Since cut determined the brilliance of the diamonds a bit more than their clarity, the diamond jewellery of the competitors 'dazzled' as much as Tanishq's but were much cheaper. 'I was from the industry; I knew all this. I took the help of two colleagues from manufacturing and sourcing (the VS-GH supplies were also better than the VVS-GH) and argued the case for VS-GH with the leaders and made us move away from the holy cow of VVS-GH!' Bharat exults. This was a significant move. The subsequent move into the SI grade in 2013 would take Tanishq even deeper into the diamond jewellery territory.

While all these were exciting things to be part of, without a doubt, the pressure on the leaders must have been high. Your customers are unhappy. Your team members are stressed out. Your board expects you to fail but feels sorry for you. In such a situation, how do you *will* yourself to go to the office every day, *where is your source of motivation?*

Even though Jacob and I were just two floors away in the same building, our work lives were keeping us busy, with hardly any opportunity for interaction and an occasional bumping into each other in the elevator. So, I had no clue how Jacob was coping. 'Every time I felt down, I would go to the factory. The people there had so much idealism, so much faith, so much commitment and a sense of duty. I would go and talk to them for an hour, and I would be totally rejuvenated!' Jacob seems to be energized even today by the recollection.

One good thing that happened was the induction of new senior staff in the division, bringing with them considerably fresh perspectives as well. Govind Raj, who was heading Retail, was the right salve that was needed for the damaged balance sheets and egos of the franchisee partners. Saroja who was heading Marketing was the feisty intellectual with a penchant for innovation, what the customer and market challenges called for. And Harish Bhat, who moved in 2001 from Tata Tea, as VP of Sales and Marketing, just as the brand and business were coming out of the woods, brought systems, processes and scale-thinking.

I remember hearing the news about Harish and feeling disappointed, even angry. By then Tanishq was turning around and that VP's position, pitched higher than my general-manager level in the Watches division, was underscoring that status change. Moreover, Harish was to be a deputy to Jacob, whom I had worked exceedingly well with. In a few weeks I had got over my disappointment but it must have rankled deep down. A year or so later when Jacob was at the same lunch table with me, I expressed my discontent in an unguarded moment. Immediately, I cursed myself for my carelessness and for putting him in a spot. Ever the gentleman, Jacob replied, 'I was pretty sure that the Watches division would not release you, so I had to go out.'

Harish Bhat, who recently retired as the brand custodian at Tata Sons and continues to be a director in many Tata companies, joined Tanishq in 2001 and recollects attending his first BAM in Fort Aguada, Goa. The theme was 'Let's believe!' Harish describes a rousing speech made by Jacob at this conference. It was quite apparent that Jacob was working to win the battle in the minds first. Many franchisees in the audience were doubtful, the result of five years of struggle. But, through that riveting, soul-stirring speech around belief, nationalism and Tanishq on the world stage, Jacob eliminated all the sceptics that day. Harish recollects not one, but many rounds of standing ovation.

The first year of Jacob's leadership ended on a high, a break-even financial performance. After many years of losses, Tanishq made a profit of Rs 2 crore in FY 2000–01, on sales of Rs 200 crore. It was a clear case of snatching victory from the jaws of defeat. 'It was a big relief for all of us. We no longer had our backs to the wall. We started focusing on customers and sales.' Jacob's relief is palpable even after twenty years.

No one is more dangerous than a person with nothing left to lose. I have come across this phrase many times and it applies to business and teams as well. When you are in a tight spot, absolutely in a corner and the only way you can go is up, you should take risks, you should take a huge leap of faith. That's what the team did on multiple fronts.

Elizabeth Mathan was the head of Design for Tanishq for about five years, starting in 2001. She recollects being asked to design the crowns for the Femina Miss India contest. It was in 2003 or 2004. She had put three designers on the job, and they had created some stunning designs. She had chosen three of them to be presented to Femina. The Tanishq marketing team made the presentation to Femina and came back saying that the client felt that these were too modern, and they wanted something conventional. Elizabeth shares, 'I was very unhappy. I went to Harish Bhat and said these are fabulous designs. I am not going to redesign any. We should go back to Femina and convince them to take these. Ask them, if they want conventional designs, then why come to Tanishq? The team went back and pushed. Femina took our original designs!'

In a subjective matter like design, it's easy for the customer to dismiss the ideas or prototypes with a sweeping, 'It's too modern'. The creators need to have a strong point of view and stay firm in their belief. That belief makes the customers pause and wonder if they have missed seeing something. Without a strong customer value proposition, there is no competitive advantage. Without a strong point of view, there is no strong customer value proposition. So, every department should stay committed to its point of view, generating a kind of 'creative tension' all around, till it is settled through a professional discussion and debate. The best emerges through such a process.

Amid all the pressure that the teams were going through, there were comic episodes as well. Here was one. Aanchal Jain, who had joined Saroja's team in 2000, recollects the language ad versions of the 19 = 22 campaign. The headline – 'There's a Thief in Your Family' – had come up in 1997, playing on the word *family* in the family jeweller term. But the English words sort of softened the sting of the message.

The word *chor* in Hindi (and in other Indian languages) had an evocation that the English word *thief* lacked. So, Aanchal wrote the headline brief in Hindi (*Tumhare Ghar Mein Chor Hai!*) and gave it to the ad agency for translating into Bengali and releasing that small ad just below the gold rate on the front page in *Anandabazar Patrika*. She had come early to the office the next day. The landline rang and it was Dwaipayan Sen, the regional manager of Tanishq in Kolkata, hollering on the phone, wanting to talk to Saroja, Aanchal's boss. He was shouting, 'They are throwing stones at our store!' Aanchal initially thought he was being metaphorical, getting carried away in his anxiety. After talking to him for a couple of minutes, she realized that some people were literally throwing stones at the Camac Street store! Aanchal is hysterical as she shares this with me, obviously having left those tensions behind two decades ago!

There were other milestones and innovations not just in the manufacturing and marketing side but also in the adoption of financial programmes and schemes. 'I was blown away when Bhaskar Bhat told me sometime recently that the greatest gift I gave Titan was Gold-On-Lease,' says Anto or Antony Motha, who headed the commercial function of Tanishq during the period. He was talking about the transformational credit line that he (and Keerthivasan, another colleague of his) enabled the Titan Company to get in 2001. Rajarathnam, who was a leader in the corporate finance team at that time, was also involved in getting this innovation on board.

Prior to this, all gold was being purchased from banks or customers (through the exchange programme). After this purchase, there was a price risk. Let's say, Titan bought 10 kilograms of gold on 1 January at Rs 500 per gram and gave that gold to the vendors to make jewellery; it took a month for this jewellery to be made and assume that the price of gold fell to Rs 475 per gram on 1 February when Titan sold all that jewellery to customers. This would have meant that Titan lost 5 per cent on that sale, which is a big loss in a business like jewellery. There are 'hedging' mechanisms in commodity businesses that help manage this risk effectively, but those were not available for gold at that time. So, Titan was sitting on a big risk. Of course, Titan could benefit as well, if the selling price in this situation was Rs 525 per gram instead of Rs 475. But that was a gamble, and certainly not worth building the business around.

Titan desperately needed a solution.

All the central banks of the world hold hundreds of tonnes of gold, as gold is the ultimate hedge for governments as well. This gold is held in physical form and as such does not provide any return. The central banks release part of the physical stocks to international bullion banks, who 'lease' that gold to jewellery manufacturers at low rates of interest. Part of that interest income is kept by the bullion banks and the rest goes back to the central banks, who end up making some money on their gold reserves.

This is how the Gold-on-Lease (GOL) programme was created. It had been available in India in a limited way, but it was not well known.

Anto and Keerthivasan came to know about GOL sometime in 2002 and they started it first with Commerzbank. Titan got 180 days of credit from the bank, and the price could be fixed any day before the one hundred and eightieth day of purchase, which meant that Titan could match the sale price and purchase price of all its gold. The GOL interest was less than 2 per cent per annum, compared to working capital costs that were many times that. Anto recollects that Mr Ishaat Hussain (Titan's board director at that time) blessed it in the board meeting confirming that it was a form of legitimate credit.

GOL has continued to power the growth of Tanishq over the next two decades, enabling Tanishq to use low-cost, risk-free credit to open stores in big cities and the smallest of towns across India.

Another transformational programme that continues till today is the Golden Harvest jewellery purchase programme. This was a jewellery purchase scheme where a customer paid equal installments for eleven months and Tanishq topped it up with one installment at the end of the twelfth month, after which the customer gets a substantial sum to buy jewellery that she would not have been able to buy with a full down-payment. Typically, the customer ends up spending at least 50 per cent more on the 'saved amount' when she makes the purchase. Most customers time the closure of the Golden Harvest Scheme (GHS) to important events in their lives, including big festivals like Dhanteras and Akshaya Tritiya.

Chennai jewellers already had similar schemes and many in the Tanishq team were not convinced. The leadership teams' minds were eventually changed when the Kozhikode Tanishq franchisee persisted with them on this and finally convinced them to start a similar programme which ended up as the GHS. The GHS now contributes to nearly a fifth of the sales of Tanishq.

While all this was happening, Tanishq continued to do well in FY 2001–02, achieving sales of Rs 268 crore and a Rs 2.3 crore profit, second year running. Belief was starting to come in from the Titan board's side and from Tata Sons as well.

Ireena Vittal was part of McKinsey & Co. in 2001 when the consulting firm was given the portfolio strategy assignment by Titan Company. 'We were engaged by Titan, but the trigger was clearly from Tata Sons,' recalls Ireena. After sixteen years of being the MD, Xerxes Desai was about to retire in March 2002 and Bhaskar Bhat was taking over. Titan was cleaning up the balance sheet

Promotional material for the Golden Harvest Scheme, a programme that spoke to the deep desire within Indians to economize and save

after deciding to exit the European watch operation and write off the losses. Ireena remembers that two questions remained. The first was a question about Titan's portfolio: Should Titan shrink back to watches? The second was to answer a specific question posed by Mr Ratan Tata (RNT): Why should the Tatas give their name to a category like gold?

McKinsey's belief in the jewellery business came from three points. One, the jewellery industry was huge. Two, the formalizing of the industry was clearly in the works, with hundreds of mom-and-pop jewellers giving way to large regional players. Three, while there was a large part of it which was near-commodity in nature with a low-margin profile, there was adequate and growing space for design differentiation and high-margin jewellery. The one big switch in their mind was that Tanishq, being in the low gross-margin jewellery category, should define itself as a retailer, while it was okay for Titan (the watch business), being in the high gross-margin watches category, to see itself as a product business. This was a big shift the Tanishq team had to make, with Return on Capital Employed (ROCE) becoming a critical objective. With these points, McKinsey recommended to Tata Sons that Titan Company should continue with Tanishq.

'I told Bhaskar that I will go first,' Jacob is referring

to the legendary Business Review Committee (BRC) meeting of Tata Sons in Mumbai in 2002, where he told Bhaskar (who had taken over as MD, Titan, on 1 April 2002) that the watches presentation can follow his presentation on Tanishq! It was clearly the risk-taking man at work! 'I made a presentation of the turnaround in the business, the many new things we were doing, the large opportunity in front of us and made an impassioned appeal to the BRC,' Jacob says. 'Then Gautam Kumra of McKinsey asks RNT, "*Mr Tata, what do you think of this business?*" There's a studied silence from Mr Tata, after which he responds that the business seemed to be doing well and that the board should give it more time.' Jacob's relief was palpable. 'I called the team back home, who were all waiting with bated breath, to give them the great news.'

After that crucial meeting, Tanishq went from strength to strength. Over the next three years, operations strengthened, innovation accelerated and employee and partner morale exploded. Sales crossed Rs 400 crore in FY 2003–04, which was more than 40 per cent of Titan Company's total sales, and profits topped Rs 14 crore, fourth-year profitability running. All-round belief and conviction also came with all those significant, sustained milestones.

Titan's annual report for FY 2003–04 signals this:[8]

While the previous year saw a relentless search for viability resulting in a successful turnaround of the business, this year marked the beginning of a confident march towards prosperity . . . sales value increasing by over 23% and profitability registering a handsome increase by over 160% . . . With annual growth rates in revenues exceeding 35% over the past four years, Tanishq is also one of the fastest growing consumer businesses in the country.

Jacob left Titan sometime in the middle of 2003 and Harish Bhat took over as the COO. *'What made you leave Titan?'* I ask Jacob. 'Ah, let's not talk about that now, Venkat. That's for another book!' Jacob chuckles.

Antony Motha says that Jacob was the inspiring leader who was needed when everyone had to be pulled out of the doldrums and get energized. And then Harish Bhat took over in 2003 when we needed a leader like him, when we needed systems and processes for growth, for building scale. The point that Anto makes is a very perceptive one. Different types of leaders are needed at different stages in an organization's journey. When things were bad, like it was with Tanishq in 2000, we needed a personality who could take risky bets, galvanize the teams towards the goals, drive everyone like a demon, pull absolutely no punches, suffer no fools and be fearless to stand alone. Jacob was that. Then comes a stage when systematic planning of operations, organizing all departments around key milestones, defining clear KRAs and KPIs, building a strong review process and building consensus become essential. Harish was the leader who could implement that and build the foundations for scale, thus, enabling Tanishq to grow further in store network and sales. An intra-Tata Group transfer (he was from the Tata Administrative Services cadre) took him out of Titan in January 2005.

Meanwhile, sales of Tanishq crossed Rs 490 crore in FY 2004–05 and profits crossed the Rs 16 crore mark. The tone of the annual report of FY 2004–05 was very confident:[9]

> The division's income has more than doubled, from Rs 243 crore to Rs 493 crore, in the short span of three years ... The enhanced desirability of the brand Tanishq enabled us to improve our retail margins. This, along with reduced costs consequent to greater economies of scale, worked in tandem to enhance our operating margins...

The orbit shift had occurred. When the Jewellery division won the JRD Quality Value Award (a prestigious milestone as part of the Tata Group Business Excellence programme) in 2012, Bhaskar Bhat recollects that RNT was graceful as always. He remarked on how far Tanishq had come and that 'Xerxes has been proven right, and we were wrong'.

3

On Cruise Control: 2005–2013

I joined Titan in May of 1990 as the advertising manager and remained in the marketing function of the Watches division for more than a decade. Between 1997 and 2000, Jacob had been my boss. I became the head of marketing of the Watches division in early 2000, when Jacob was made the chief strategy officer of the company, as mentioned in the last chapter.

In June or July 2000, I decided to leave Titan. My rationale is lost in the mists of time. I had just become the boss of Marketing, with Jacob moving to head strategy for the company, so I should have had every reason for staying in Titan. Perhaps I was a bit bored, maybe there was a feeling of under-achievement with a couple of years of stagnation in the Watches division's business in India.

I was to join Levi Strauss India to head their Marketing. After soaking in that idea for a few weeks, I put in my papers and was ready to start something new.

Bijou Kurien, my boss at that time, and Bhaskar Bhat, the COO of Watches, tried to reason with me. The logical arguments were there: I had already built my reputation; Titan was a large, successful company; Tata Group had so much to offer and so on. But I was not swayed. The global, fashion aspect of Levi's was heady. I remained firm. Or so I thought. When I was counting down to my last few weeks in Titan, Mr Desai called me into his room one day. It was a Friday. As soon as I went in, he took off on me. He was not loud, but quite intense, angry. 'How dare you leave the family? Surely, we can discuss and sort out whatever issue you have, just like you do within a family! Get out of my room now, take a break for a few days. Tell those people you are not joining them and come and tell me you are back for good. Now go!' He literally threw me out of the room. I came out, jolted. I was unsettled, confused, worried. All the excitement and confidence of living out my future in the 501s and Red Loops evaporated in an instant. Family! How can I leave my family? I started brooding over this for the next few hours until I called Levi's HR manager later in the evening to tell her that I would not be joining them, because of a last-minute change of mind. She was understandably upset at my late decision.

Titan had always been an excellent company for me. However, surely there were other fine companies in this world, including Levi's. I could leave one, join another and rebuild in a couple of years. But when he used the word *family*, it turned everything around. Of course, Titan was family, how could I have forgotten that? And how could I leave *family*?

When I came back the next Monday, I waited until I heard that Mr Desai had come in to work and went to meet him. I told him that I wasn't leaving family and was staying back for good. He smiled that knowing smile of his and that was that.

Around mid 2003, three years after this event, the Watches division went through a restructuring and changed from a functional organization on the customer-facing side to a business unit organization with profit responsibility. Till then the sales and marketing functions were separate and their heads (I was the marketing head) reported directly to Bijou Kurien, COO of Watches. A more effective go-to-market structure felt needed, with greater profit accountability as well. Two strategic business units (SBUs) were formed, one for the Titan brand and the other for Sonata (the mass-market brand that had been launched in the mid 1990s). I was made the head of the Titan SBU, responsible for Sales, Retailing and Marketing. I had not done even a single day of selling in my life and here I was – responsible for the entire sales of the Titan brand, the mainstay of Titan Company at that time!

Because of the enabling environment of Titan Company and a supportive team, I adjusted well to the new role, my freshness of approach compensating for the total lack of experience. For about eighteen months, I was fulfilling this role quite well.

In December 2004, I think it was the 7th or 8th, I received an SMS that would change my life forever. That memory is still vivid. My office used to be on the seventh floor in Golden Enclave, close to the old airport in Bengaluru, where the Titan Company HQ had been since 1992. I used to reach the office quite early. My home was just 2 kilometres away and I used to cycle to work. The SMS came from Bijou Kurien. It read: *Harish Bhat is leaving Titan for another Tata company.*

It must have been around 8:15 a.m. It did not take me more than a minute to type back: *Dear Bijou, I want Harish's job.*

I met Bijou and Bhaskar (MD) later that day and shared my strong desire for that role. Over the next week, I persisted with them through one or two more interactions. It took them a couple of weeks to decide and my 2004 Christmas gift came to me in Bhaskar's room when Bijou called me from Kochi to give me the news, as Bhaskar smiled at me from his desk. I was going to head Tanishq as the COO! I moved into that position on 16 January 2005 and continued till 30 September 2019.

The first significant exercise I got involved in was brand positioning.

The advertising of Tanishq in the early 2000s was essentially jewellery-collection-led and had a look which was very distinctive, stylish and fashionable. The women shown were quite Western in their styling, they exhibited a behaviour which was independent and modern and the overall look and feel of the Tanishq ads were quite different from the rest of the industry. Tanishq stood out distinctively because of that. But our positioning also had some drawbacks. The brand consultant and social commentator Santosh Desai (we also went to college together) was commissioned by Tanishq sometime in 2004 to create a sustainable brand value proposition. 'I remember Harish Bhat telling me about a brand problem that needed solving. Tanishq was a highly regarded brand, well thought of, but did not seem to reside in the heart of the jewellery market – the wedding market. Tanishq was seen as good for the trinkety stuff and did not appeal to those who went to the traditional jewellers. Admired but not bought to the same extent,' he says. Santosh recollects that there was some internal conflict as well, in his view, where the brand and design teams thought of the wedding market as a business necessity, but their natural impulse was to see Tanishq for its design differentiation and fashion quotient. He remembers images of African–American women modelling for Tanishq, a woman in a TV film tossing the diamonds into the swimming pool – the team's lens of fashion leading the brand into such territories of expression.

Santosh and his team looked at various jewellery stores, spoke to Usha Balakrishnan, a jewellery historian, consulted Devdutt Pattanaik, a mythologist and author, got a semiotician on board, and did a fair amount off deep consumer conversations. After much thinking and reflection, Santosh's inputs to the Tanishq team were the following:

You are remaining outside the culture. You are behaving like an outsider. You think of jewellery as fashion. Jewellery is not fashion, Jewellery is culture. So, don't look down on tradition, don't run away from it. In fact, become the biggest repository of tradition. Yet you are Tanishq, not like any other jeweller. You are a national brand,

Ad for Chain Mela, an exhibition of different kinds of gold chains. The Tanishq ads always had a standout quality.

not a regional jeweller. So, reinvent tradition, revitalize tradition. Engage with tradition with understanding and respect. But do your own take on it!

I remember these inputs rather well as they came sometime in early 2005 after I had become the COO. While a layman may not understand some of these finer aspects of brand value propositions, many of these observations would resonate with Indians. 'Tanishq's take on tradition' immediately appealed to me. I was fresh into the category and did not know its codes well enough, but just the difference between the advertising of every other jeweller and Tanishq suggested to me that we were playing in a small field. We needed to widen the appeal of Tanishq if we wanted to grow rapidly and become a prominent player, if not the leader. The revitalizing-tradition approach seemed to have the potential to substantially widen Tanishq's appeal without diluting its unique identity. This made special sense at a time when Tanishq's sales were around Rs 500 crore in a market which was approximately Rs 50,000 crore There was so much scope for growth!

The other substantive point this fork-in-the-road moment raised was: *a brand is far too important to be left in the hands of the brand manager.* In consumer businesses, the proposition of the brand defines the scope of its play in the industry and that decision cannot be abrogated to a brand manager, likening the brand strategy to 'some ads'. It is the CEO's responsibility and duty.

The first TV film that expressed this new proposition is also one of the best Tanishq films of all time. RamSam (Rajesh Ramaswamy) is now an independent filmmaker and was the creative director at Lintas in 2005. 'We struggled for a few weeks in trying to crack our first film to communicate Revitalising Tradition,' recollects RamSam, on a Zoom call we are on, joined by Sudhir, his business partner and the head of the Tanishq account in Lintas for many years. After struggling to create a solid screenplay, the Lintas team hit pay dirt after Vikram Satyanath, the account planner on the team, came back after seeing Vidya Balan's movie *Parineeta* and suggested that they create a period setting.

That idea gave birth to the launch of the New Tales of Tradition campaign, with the film showcasing an early twentieth-century wealthy Bengali household with all its traditions, but with a twist: a demure-looking daughter-in-law wearing an exquisite kundan necklace, her *ghunghat* (veil) in place, is shown as being respectful to her in-laws, praying in the puja room, playing with her young son, and then taking over the wheel of their vintage car to the amusement of her indulgent husband and approving mother-in-law, watching from the first-floor window. The ad film was a hit and helped establish the new direction that would continue for a very long time. It would always be referred to as the 'Parineeta film' among some of us and the Lintas folks.

This approach took Tanishq soon into a serious sponsorship of Hindi movies as well. While Tanishq had signed up with *Paheli* in 2005, a Rani Mukerji–Shah Rukh Khan film, the first big one was *Jodhaa Akbar* in 2008, an Aishwarya Rai–Hrithik Roshan film, set in the Rajput–Mughal period. We ended up working with vendor partners and *karigar*s in Rajasthan and creating exquisite *kundan* jewellery for the heroine, the hero and some other characters in the film (everyone in the film except the horses and elephants, we used to joke!).

Jodhaa Akbar was a big hit and brought Tanishq to the centre of the jewellery market. The immediate success was the sale of the products inspired by the movie. But the more lasting benefits were the revival of the craft of *kundan* jewellery (exquisite Bikaneri jewellery set with stunning *polki* stones – flat-cut diamonds – and embellished with beautiful enamelling on the back of the products). And the subsequent launch of glass *kundan* jewellery, where the glass was used in the place of the *polkis* to make the jewellery affordable and accessible. Hundreds and thousands of customers have had the privilege of wearing such stunning pieces over the years.

Our next big project was weddings. Work had begun in the early 2010s to address the wedding market. Multiple communities had been identified which contributed significantly to the overall wedding jewellery sales: Telugus, Punjabis, Gujaratis, Bengalis. The multiple items that went into each trousseau were pinned down and developed with expert vendor partners. The response was good. Thousands of stock keeping units (SKUs) at the community and sub-community level were created with vendor support and stocked in the right stores. We also needed to tell all those customers that Tanishq was into serious bridal jewellery. And for that, we wanted a breakthrough TV film.

It was 2013 and the early days of our Wedding Campaign journey. After multiple scripts around conventional, feel-good situations, Lintas suddenly brought the second marriage film to the marketing team. The first version of this idea was set in a court. It was designed as a civil marriage. Deepika Tewari headed Tanishq Marketing for eight years till 2019 and recollects that her initial reaction to this idea was a bit shaky. Here they were trying to get Tanishq to be considered favourably as a brand for bridal jewellery, and Lintas wanted to present the brand in a second marriage setting! But Lintas persisted with the idea and came up with the final version, set in a conventional wedding setting. 'By then, we were starting to warm up to the boldness of the theme and were convinced about it,' adds Deepika. The film starts by showing a beautiful young woman playing with a little girl, while dressing up for a big occasion. Their relationship appears quite close, and the viewers are left thinking that the little girl is perhaps the young woman's niece. Soon it is revealed to the viewers that it is the young woman's wedding. We see the young woman and the bridegroom doing the *saat phera*s (the seven sacred rounds that a bride and groom take around the holy fire in a Hindu wedding). The little girl is sitting on the lap of the young woman's mother (ostensibly) while the *saat phera*s are happening. Suddenly, she shouts, 'Momma, I also want to do round-round!' revealing to the audience that the young woman is her mother. The young woman, a bit embarrassed, tries to shush her. But the bridegroom calls out to the little girl, carries her in his arms and the three of them complete the *saat phera*s together. The film ends with a close-up of the three of them with the little girl asking the bridegroom, '*Aaj se Daddy bulaaoon?*' ('Shall I call you Daddy from today?')

That film gave a sanction to women to do things that society unfairly frowned upon. Even in 2013, it would have been perfectly fine for a man to get married the second time, but not so easy for a woman, and barely for a woman with a child! A woman director, Gauri Shinde, made the film and her inputs made a huge difference in the overall mood and detailing. Many of these nuances – the dusky complexion of the heroine, her not wearing a *ghunghat*, the groom appearing to be younger than her – were picked up and appreciated by the viewers later. The Second Marriage film established the progressiveness and boldness of Tanishq. The film did not help us in selling the jewellery collection we had lined up at that time, but became the symbol of what Tanishq stood for.

Brand propositions like 'Revitalizing Tradition' have a long shelf life and they should be nurtured. One thing that helps in that is the continuity of the senior folks. We were lucky to have that in me and Sandeep Kulhalli (SVP of Retail and Marketing), Deepika Tewari in Tanishq and Balki and Joe and RamSam at Lowe Lintas. That's how the Second Marriage film, clearly another expression of the 'Revitalizing Tradition' proposition, was still being created eight years after the proposition was originally adopted. The proposition muscle of a brand builds through such consistent messaging.

Over the next many years, the Revitaling Tradition proposition substantially defined the flagship store strategy and the new product collection strategy of Tanishq. From about 2002, the stores of Tanishq had been opened up. Instead of the marble facades which hid the store from the street, glass had been introduced, so that you could see into the stores from the sidewalks. The interiors had become more like a store and less like an art gallery, with a greater emphasis on product display. The store staff had also left behind their 'formal' attitude. From around 2010, the store design approach started including 'local craft'. Balaji Natarajan and Chitti Babu were the store design and visual merchandizing leaders of Tanishq from the early 2000s to today. It's under their imagination that these transformations started happening.

In the flagship stores, the 'craft store' approach brought alive the traditions of a city in a way that connected deeply with the customers of that city, while retaining an aspiration through the elegance and sophistication of the execution. The Camac Street, Kolkata, store of 2012, for example, paid homage to the *palki* wedding traditions of Bengal and the architectural aspects of Victorian Kolkata. Any Bengali would have felt at home as soon as they entered the store. At the same time, the premium styling

Traditional Bengali 'palki' wedding mural on the wall of the Camac Street store in Kolkata

and detailing of the store was unmistakable, to sustain the brand aspiration and desire.

Between 2005 and 2013, we did many other things that took Tanishq to the centre of the jewellery market.

GHS Redux

We were on the terrace of the Royal Orchid Hotel in Bengaluru on a chill winter evening. I think it was 2006. Head of Tanishq Retail, Saumen Bhaumik, and Ajay Sharma, who had recently joined Titan as the head of Commercial for Jewellery division, had joined me in a corner of the terrace. We were all nursing our first drink. Ajay Sharma was extremely anxious. 'How can we make money on gold jewellery when we are giving away such a big discount, making the cost of sales 8.33 per cent?' Ajay was dubious of our '11+1' GHS programme. The GHS had been in existence for a while, where the customers paid eleven monthly instalments and the company topped it up with one instalment at the end and the customer could buy jewellery with those twelve instalments. The 8.33 per cent referred to that *one bonus paid by the company on the twelve of sales (1÷12×100%)*. So, Ajay's question had merit. *At least on the face of it.* But Saumen Bhaumik was made of sterner stuff. After more than ten years in jewellery manufacturing, he had moved to head Retail at Tanishq (Saumen is now CEO of the Eyecare division). He recognized the deep Indian desire for saving and the potential explosive power of the GHS. So Saumen was not about to let this go. 'But we will be securing the future of the business. Also, all customers end up buying much more than what they deposited. Also, it's another method of customer acquisition, with a cost that compares well with advertising . . .' Over the next few glasses of Old Monk, the dots started to connect, my rookie naivete adding to the debate.

We realized that the 'upselling' was nearly 80 per cent, meaning that if a customer saved up Rs 12,000 over twelve months (including the bonus we gave), she would invariably end up buying jewellery worth approximately Rs 20,000, so the cost of sales was not 1/12, but 1/20. We also realized that we had forgotten to value the interest income from the customer cash flows, which would sit in our bank. By the time the fifth glass was finished, we had brought these key aspects into the economics and the cost of sales had dropped from 8.33 per cent to under 3 per cent and looked quite comparable to advertising as a method of customer acquisition. Even Ajay Sharma was convinced now. All three of us were excited about the conversation and the outcome.

Soon after this, Saumen travelled far and wide across the country. He exhorted every store manager, every franchisee partner and all the store staff about the power of securing future sales and how the GHS should be pitched to every person walking into the store, irrespective of their profile. His passion created many believers. Like Vilas Kale, our franchisee partner in Nagpur. Vilas and his staff went all out to sign up GHS members. And a powerful insight emerged – it was not only the middle class who liked to save; even the rich wanted to do that. Monthly instalments started as low as Rs 2,000 and crossed even the Rs 1 lakh mark! Other cities and stores took up similar efforts and, soon, the overall results were huge, with 30, 40 and 50 per cent of the next year's sales already signed up by some benchmark stores. Everyone was caught up in the national fever of GHS enrollment and redemption. Saumen went hammer and tongs behind this programme over the next few years to make it a huge engine of growth for Tanishq, and a big industry practice over time.

New Shoots

The focus on diamond jewellery began in 2006.

Multiple actions were undertaken from early 2006 to scale up the diamond jewellery business in a big way.

Diamond jewellery would help build the desire for the brand and would also deliver better profits. For instance, one: widening the use of VS clarity as well as using much smaller diamonds (the costs of smaller diamonds were disproportionately lower than the costs of larger diamonds: a 1-cent stone VS would cost disproportionately less than what a 2-cent VS stone would cost, assuming it's the same cut and colour). This helped us make affordable diamond jewellery (less than Rs 1 lakh) at scale, bringing it to the middle class. Two: partnering with vendors and exhibiting exquisite high-value diamond jewellery in five-star hotels in metro cities and showing an impressive new face of Tanishq to wealthy customers.

To integrate all these initiatives into a single purpose, L.R. Natrajan (LRN), who had joined in 2003 as the head of jewellery manufacturing, suggested a 'Double-Studded Sales' programme which had the target of doubling diamond jewellery sales every year. Each one of these initiatives kept firing for many years and our growth in diamond jewellery clipped at an exceptional 75 per cent per year.

Today, diamond jewellery accounts *for a little over 30 per cent of* Tanishq's sales.

It was early 2010 if I recollect. The mutual respect between the Design and Merchandizing departments (the department responsible for the product strategy) in Tanishq was still in its early stages. In a meeting with both teams, I shared my thoughts on Product Strategy: 'In our business, the most important thing is the *turn*!' I paused for effect. The Merchandizing folks were elated – *this is the CEO after our hearts. He is so business-oriented, so numbers-driven!* The designers were crestfallen – *and we thought Venkat was different*! *That he was a creative guy*! After a dramatic pause, I continued, 'Our jewellery should *turn* heads. If that happens, the stock will turn!' Now it was the 'turn' of the Merchandizing folks to be disappointed and the designers to exult. My view was clear to all – differentiation should ultimately drive product and brand strategy.

The customer obsession started in 2007 and gave birth to the 'Creating Fans' programme. A high level of process orientation combined with 'heart' sought to deliver customer delight at scale and laid the foundations of one the biggest competitive advantages of Tanishq: the deep and wide knowledge about millions of customers and the deep relationship between the salesperson and the customer. The brand substantially expanded its physical reach and brought purity, design, quality and exceptional customer experience to many more towns and customers. Hisar, Jalandhar, Aligarh, Allahabad, Muzaffarpur,

Agartala, Guntur, Aurangabad, Anand, Mysore and many others opened their doors to the new experience in jewellery. The GOL facility laid the foundation for the rapid expansion of Tanishq stores into small-town India.

We were on the road all the time, keeping in touch with our sales staff and franchisee partners, and visiting other jewellers wherever we went. We soaked in all the learning like a sponge and created our versions of effective processes and policies, making Tanishq much stronger as a result.

Three new category reach-outs also took place in these years.

Influenced by the perception that the Tanishq brand would continue to be out of reach for the middle class and small-town India, 'Gold Plus from Tata' was conceived and launched in 2005 by LRN and a team drawn from factory employees. It was a new brand, more traditional in its design style, lower priced and more South Indian in its personality. Rooted in tradition and personalization, Gold Plus started very well and planted its roots deeply in the small towns of Tamil Nadu, Telangana, Andhra Pradesh and Karnataka. Gold Plus achieved reasonable success in the first five years. But with the entry of the large South jewellers into those towns, its inability to build a strong customer value proposition and Tanishq's own growing middle-class pull, the raison d'être for Gold

Plus started diminishing in early 2010. Gold Plus was finally subsumed into the Tanishq brand by 2016.

Zoya, a luxury jewellery brand, and Mia, a sub-brand of Tanishq for the younger woman, were launched in 2009 and 2012 respectively, with an eye on the future. Both developed very well over the next many years and became ready for explosive scale-up by 2020, creating substantial niches for themselves.

A growing confidence made us launch Tanishq in the US in 2007, aimed at mainstream American women, sidestepping the logical NRI/PIO segment. While the initial response was very satisfying, we realized that we had underestimated the long-haul nature of such a venture. The 2008 global financial crisis put a lid on that business, making us shut two of our stores and set aside our international ambitions for more than a decade.

Our consciousness about the state of jewellery manufacturing and the state of the *karigar*s (artisans) rose substantially, paving the way for a wave of programmes like Unnati, Mr Perfect, Mr Perfect+ and the Karigar Centre which would ultimately lead to a transformational impact on the industry and bind vendors and *karigar*s to Tanishq and Titan Company forever.

In the eight years between 2005 and 2013, the price of gold rose 5x and breached the Rs 3,000 mark for 1 gram of 24 karats. Since the making charges that we levied (the value addition in this business) had always been in absolute rupees, the gross contribution margin (value addition as a per cent of sales value – a very critical indicator of the health of any business) came under significant pressure. Ishaat Hussain honed in on this issue and persisted in putting pressure on me to convert the making charges into a percentage of the price of gold. His persistence resulted in the change, and we created the industry's first 'percentage making charges', changing the predictability of our profitability forever. Over these eight years, the sales of Tanishq grew 16x over to 8,000 crore. From being the loss-making business of Titan Company in 2000, the jewellery business became the majority sales and profit contributor by 2013 and the leading brand in the jewellery industry, with an influence that was visible on many fronts.

It looked like nothing could go wrong.

But we did not know what was lurking around the corner.

4

The Challenging Years and Recovery: 2013–2019

In March 2013, India's current account deficit (CAD) reached a high of 4.8 per cent of GDP, an unsustainable level. The import of gold in 2012–13 (FY 2013) was 845 tonnes and the gold import bill contributed to 50 per cent of the CAD. The Government of India clearly considered gold a nonessential import and sought to control it. Two very significant measures were brought in during June 2013. The first was that any importer of gold had to export 20 per cent of the imports (called the 80:20 rule) and get the payment within nine months. The second was the abolition of the GOL facility.

This was going to have a huge impact on Tanishq. To start with, against the 845 tonnes of gold imported into

India in FY 2013, only 70 tonnes had been exported. This meant that with the 80:20 rule in play, the total import would crash to less than 400 tonnes in FY 2014, which was the government's intention. This would squeeze the domestic supply completely and have a significant impact on our production and sales. While we had just managed to get a Direct Import License for gold in 2012 (gold was a restricted item), we had zero exports, and our license suddenly had no value. The abolition of GOL was even worse; we were dependent on the 180 days of credit through GOL, its price risk protection and had a super light balance sheet on account of that.

Keerthivasan is a Titan veteran and has been heading Gold Bullion procurement for more than twenty years. 'All our relationships totally came into play at that time. Plus, being Titan and a Tata group company was so helpful,' he recalls. Fortunately, banks could import in anticipation of orders. Some had done that and had decent stocks. We maximized the procurement from Kotak, SBI and ICICI banks during June and July of 2013, just before GOL was abolished. From July, we had to contend with the import restriction as well as the absence of GOL. The other significant help came from a copper company. Birla Copper was India's largest copper smelting company. One by-product of copper smelting was gold! Again, being

Titan and part of the Tata group helped. Birla Copper even agreed to our condition of making the payment after we melted their gold in our plant and confirmed the purity. They gave us the right of first refusal on their stocks. We bought 2 tonnes from them during FY 2014. It was a big relief!

C. Ramachandran is a general manager in Titan's Finance department today and was heading Tanishq's Finance department in those challenging years. 'For five months, there were no imports of gold. But between the stocks with the banks and Birla Copper, we ended up managing. Then there was this godsend GDS, Gold Deposit Scheme!' he smiles. GDS was the scheme through which all the temples of India deposited their gold (given by the devotees) with banks for safekeeping. SBI, being the largest bank in India had the maximum GDS stock. Our relationship with SBI and Keerthivasan's persistent efforts behind multiple SBI branches unlocked this for us. We got 3 tonnes of gold from SBI through this route, and we also got GOL for this since this was not an import. Tirupati gold accounted for much of this and was literally a blessing!

Subramaniam (Subbu) was Titan's CFO from 2011 to 2021 and vividly remembers the special call he set up with the investors about the significant change in Titan's balance sheet. Titan had financed a big part of its gold purchases in FY 2013 through GOL. Because of the abolition of GOL, Titan had to borrow that much in FY 2014 to procure its gold, leading to higher interest cost, a balance sheet with considerable debt and a much lower ROCE. In that investor call that Subbu referred to, we pictured all this for the investors for total clarity. Subbu remembers some of his peers in the industry asking him why we were being so upfront about it and his clarification to them stating how we wanted to be absolutely honest and transparent about the challenge. Subbu smiles, 'The investors remember this even today. The trust in Titan's management was built through events like this.'

The domestic jewellery market was the third largest in the world at that time and Titan had decided to focus only on domestic sales, especially after the 2008 failure in the US. There were no export sales at all in FY 2013. It was zero. We had to scramble fast and build some export business. Mohammed Mustafa in Singapore and Damas in Dubai quickly became our customers, and we started exporting jewellery in early FY 2014. Sandeep Kulhalli, a Titan veteran who retired in 2020 as the senior VP of Retail and Marketing of Titan's Jewellery division, was the man who took urgent steps to build that business. Apart from the import benefits that came with those exports, these efforts were also being noticed by the government departments which wanted companies to push exports.

These challenges taught us about the power of advocacy. Bhaskar and Subbu had gone to meet a senior RBI person about GOL. He was curt with them, almost telling them not to waste his time, that Titan should rise above its selfish interests and appreciate the country's problems, etc. They agreed with him but made the point about the need to hedge gold and how GOL had protected every manufacturer from the fluctuations in price and how Titan would miss that facility. The RBI official was struck by Titan's desire to hedge gold. Maybe he had preconceived notions about the jewellery industry. 'He then started warming up,' the satisfaction in Subbu's voice is visible even after ten years. Subbu requested him to at least permit the industry to hedge gold in the overseas markets (since the domestic commodity exchange was not developed enough in 2013). He assured him that this permission would not change any aspect of the import controls that the government wanted to keep, while providing a safety net to the industry. After some back and forth, the RBI official was convinced. Soon, thereafter, RBI issued policies that enabled international hedging of gold. For Titan and others, this dramatically reduced the gold price risk.

Creativity under Pressure

These regulatory preoccupations were not keeping us away from what we were normally used to doing though!

'But how can we keep diluting the brand like this?' was a sincere plea from one of the old-timers at Tanishq. The conversation was about diamonds and the quality used in Tanishq. We had used only VVS quality diamonds in Tanishq in the initial years and it was after considerable debate that the team moved to VS quality in 2004 or so, deepening and widening its use over the next many years.

Now it was May of 2013; we were at the cusp of launching our first breakthrough collection (but we did not know that yet). While we were doing quite well in sales and profit, the sales from our own designed collections were not yet significant. Inara was the beginning of that and the idea had come up – *why don't we use SI-quality diamonds at scale? It will give us at least a 25 per cent price benefit.* The products will be 25 per cent bigger for the same price. Great competitive advantage, terrific value for money! 'But we would be diluting the brand!' The old timers were persisting, and sincerely so.

For years, the South was the diamond capital of the country and set the standards in quality. VVS was the norm and played to the South Indians' desire to buy diamonds without any 'impurities'. For years this had fed the belief system and underscored the quality obsession of brands. But to the rule breakers, that we had become by then, there were simply no rules. The proponents of the heresy are not about to give in.

Biren Jhaveri, who has headed Diamond Procurement for Tanishq since 2009 recollects the contours of the argument from the side of the rule-breakers: *But the scintillation of a diamond is determined more by the colour and the cut. Would we not be making diamonds rather more accessible to everyone? Isn't that a great thing?* The sceptics were slowly won over by some of us batting solidly for the democratization of diamonds. A whole new beginning was made with this step in July of 2013 and the blockbuster launch of the Inara jewellery collection with SI diamonds soon followed. We started with an inventory investment of Rs 300 crore (a huge amount for a collection in 2013) and a big marketing campaign. Inara ultimately crossed Rs 500 crore in sales. The diamond jewellery business of Tanishq would never be the same again.

Inara came about because of a conversation between Revathi Kant, the head of the Tanishq Design Studio from 2010 to 2017, and a vendor partner. In August 2012, she was at the India International Jewellery Show (IIJS), Mumbai, visiting the stall of Jewel Goldi, one of our newer vendor partners. Sanjay Jaiswal, the head of Jewel Goldi, showed her a few items of jewellery placed at a small corner of the display. He told her that they had used a technique called 'nick-setting' on these items to mimic the brilliance of diamonds and those items had become fast-moving in Tanishq.

Then the PAN card rule came in 2013, where customers had to give their PAN card for every transaction of Rs 5 lakh or more. As always, necessity turned out to be the mother of invention. Revathi smiles and says, 'I said, let's make a 4.95 lakh necklace and make it look like 7 lakh!' Jewel Goldi and a few other vendors partnered with us and put together a whole line of jewellery which combined SI diamonds and the 'nick-setting' technique to create a diamond spread that was very impressive but cost less than it looked. Thus, Inara was born!

Ananthanarayanan (Ananth) was the general manager of the Merchandizing function at Tanishq between 2011 and 2017. 'My initial days were spent in understanding what we really needed,' Ananth shares. He realized that the teams needed to do two very critical but different things. The first was to bring considerable science and system into the management of the product range in every store. The second was to 'romance' the product a lot more and bring design and craft into the centre of the brand and business. We first brought a lot of science into the store assortments, where the total stock norm for each store was broken into category/weight band levels (bangles less than 10 grams, for instance) to maximize the relevant representation of products based on the customer segments that store was supposed to serve. This would minimize loss of sales and maximize stock turn, both key to retail. For instance, each bangle design was sold as a single or as a pair or as a set of four (called a UoM, Unit of Measurement). A deep understanding of the market and its culture helped in keeping the right stocks of the single/pair/set of four in every store.

Helping to maximize sales of the pair and the set of four in markets like Bihar and Odisha where customers preferred those versus Andhra Pradesh where all three UoMs were equally popular. Then conversations began with Revathi in real earnest. Can the Design department handle so many collections? How do they together bring life into refresher and gap filler products (called Core) which gave the brand the volumes? Simultaneously, they also started pushing the vendors for their innovation. Vendor Product Innovation Meets became a way of life. In no time, the Merchandizing and Design functions were standing shoulder to shoulder, creating thousands of exciting new products and multiple collections each year and the stores and customers were quite excited by the outcome. Before Inara, we were perhaps doing four to five collections a year, but with cumulative sales of about Rs 200 crore from those. With Inara, and later, we were doing a similar number of collections, but topping Rs 1,000 crore from those in a year.

On the face of it, the Design department is all about artistry and the Merchandizing department is all about science. But in the reality of business, all these black-and-whites disappear and morph into a whole world of grey tones. The designer should always be thinking, *what's the point if this necklace does not adorn a hundred necks? How do I make the sell-through (rate of sale) high? Shouldn't a more expensive bangle be more profitable than a less expensive bangle?* While the merchandizer should be bothered about, *without a deep-design story, how do we create the pull? Without the emphasis on superior craftsmanship, how do we charge a premium? Don't these statement pieces have a role in our portfolio, despite a low stock turn?* The leaders of 'opposing' teams like these two should be chosen as much for their capabilities as for their personalities. The combination of their abilities and personalities will add depth to their team and their learnings. Their different leanings will make them all diverge to start with, but the best solutions emerge through the continuous sparring of these 'opposing' forces and the convergence in their views.

The manufacturing and sourcing backbone of Tanishq was always referred to as the Integrated Supply Chain Management (ISCM) department. Something about that term always felt incomplete to me. Sometime in 2014, I was talking to the ISCM team. I told them that the term 'supply chain' evoked a very smooth movement of materials, from raw materials to work-in-process to finished goods; from a manufacturing location through warehouses to a customer location – the vivid picture evoked by that was a super-efficient conveyor belt, I told them, and wondered whether we were all focusing too much on the belt itself, its speed, its width and capacity and *sometimes forgot what was actually sitting on the belt* – the exquisite jewellery! Of course, we needed an efficient supply chain for the Network Retail Chain that we were, but we also needed a deep manufacturing capability for the *jeweller* that we also were! Over the years, considerable investments have gone into technology, people and vendors partnering to build that capability.

Luckily, FY 2014 passed much better than we thought. We somehow managed the gold supplies and production, hedged the gold overseas and grew in sales by around 8 per cent over FY 2013, which was pretty good, given the circumstances. Towards the end of that financial year, the government's view on imports had softened, after the CAD had been brought under control. We started thinking again about the scorching pace of growth that we were used to. But, once again, we barely knew what was in store for us.

As shared earlier, the GHS, started in the early 2000s, had become a powerful force in our business by then, contributing to 30 per cent of Tanishq's sales by FY 2014. That was close to Rs 3000 crore of sales, which was very substantial. This scheme recognized the innate Indian desire to save up for buying something big and had worked on that opportunity assiduously over the last decade. Many other jewellers had similar schemes as well.

In the two years before 2014, there were a few 'chit' funds across the country that had collapsed, run by opportunistic finance companies luring gullible investors with very attractive returns. Tens of thousands of people had lost their life's savings. The government had to take note of this and act in the interest of the public, which it did. Sometime in March 2014, the new rules under the Companies Act were notified, which had troubling implications for the jewellery industry. The government intended to regulate multiple 'finance' schemes across the board and the rules seemed to include the jewellery purchase schemes as well.

'I went through the new Company Law notifications

and concluded that we are going to be hit big time!' says Subbu, Titan's CFO at that time. Subbu went to the Ministry of Corporate Affairs to double check. On his first visit, he was told that jewellery schemes were not covered by this notification. But he wanted to be certain. Then, Subbu and I both went to Delhi to seek further clarification and we were informed that schemes like GHS would also be covered. The impact of that was huge. From 1 April 2014, we had to stop enrolling any new GHS accounts. By 31 August 2014, we had to complete redeeming all existing accounts. By 31 March 2015, we had to have zero balances from the existing scheme. For any future scheme, we needed shareholder approval and the total amount we could collect was capped at 25 per cent of the company's net worth. The rate of return was capped at 12 per cent per annum (*the existing GHS had an imputed 16.66 per cent*). With this, multiple guardrails had been brought in.

FY 2015 was quite eventful. We had to deal with many legal and regulatory issues around GHS closure. Innumerable customers needed to be dealt with, and much explanation had to be given to them. And we had to simultaneously build a new scheme from scratch, energizing a sales team that had got rusty with many months of not enrolling a single account. Subbu and team were working on the regulator/shareholder side and Sandeep Kulhalli and team were working on the front, with hundreds of stores and thousands of staff. By the end of FY 2015, we had done much better than we had expected at the beginning of the year. We had accomplished everything that the regulation wanted us to do, plus got the shareholders' permission for a new scheme, launched it and had started enrolling new accounts by December 2014. But the momentum that GHS had helped Tanishq achieve had been lost. Sales from GHS, which had been close to Rs 3,000 crore in FY 2014, crashed to less than Rs 500 crore in FY 2016 and would reach the FY 2014 absolute levels only by FY 2020. And because GHS had been such a driving force in the growth of Tanishq, the overall sales growth of Tanishq slowed down as well: FY 2018 was just 1.5x of FY 2014 sales, compared to the 2.5x, 4.4x and 3x for the preceding three 4-year periods going back from FY 2014 to FY 2002.

The Management Discussion and Analysis section of the FY 2016 Annual Report had this to say:[10]

Demand

The performance of the Jewellery Division in the last 3 years needs to be seen in the context of several market and regulatory events that have impacted the jewellery industry in India. Multiple structural factors have played out inside and around the industry, having a lasting impact on supply and demand. These are:

Regulatory

1. The introduction of the 80/20 rule for gold imports, the abolition of the Gold-On-Lease scheme and the subsequent reversal of both
2. The increasing of customs duty to 10%
3. The circumscribing of jewellery purchase schemes to 25% of company net worth and the capping of interest rate to 12%
4. The lowering of the PAN card limit for purchased to Rs 2 lakhs, as opposed to the Rs 5 lakhs limit that had prevailed since 2011
5. The introduction of excise duty

But regulatory challenges or not, we had to continue building our strategies for the future.

In fact, the quality of resilience is a key requirement for an organization, particularly its leaders. While we were getting hit with one regulatory shock after another, we were mature enough to take it in our stride and not let those swamp us. Of course, we had to do many things to get over those challenges, but we did not let them cramp the breadth and depth of our strategic thrust. The biggest reason for this was that we remained calm. In the corporate world, we use the words pressure and stress interchangeably. 'Oh god, there is so much pressure at work!', 'The stress is killing me!' I would argue that the words mean two entirely different things.

In the diamond business, there is a powerful phrase: 'No pressure, no diamonds.' I believe that it applies to the workplace in general. What do I mean by that? Pressure is what challenges put on us, pressure is what creates the bridge between the potential for innovation and the actual strategy. Pressure is what all of us should use to thrive and succeed. Stress is when you are not embracing the pressure that is current but have fast-forwarded into the future to contemplate failure. The possibility of failure starts occupying more of your mind-space than the actual solving of the challenge and this creates and amplifies the anxiety and generates stress, which is dysfunctional.

Embrace the pressure; throw out the stress. It takes effort to achieve this, but it is possible.

Divyam

By the time the GHS shock came, the gold import and GOL regulatory pressure had given us considerable experience. And that's how, even amid the GHS action, we were about to start our even bigger product collection effort!

'Revathi, why are you focusing our Diwali collection efforts on gold jewellery?' This had been my refrain to Revathi and her colleague Anjali Sikka on their repeated attempts to convince Sandeep Kulhalli, VP of Retail and Marketing, and me to launch a gold collection for Diwali. Revathi did not relent. She was quite blunt, 'You may be focusing on profits, Venkat, but I am focusing on customers!' This telling observation paved the way for the launch of Divyam in 2015 season – our first gold collection for Diwali.

Fusion of multiple techniques was at the centre of Divyam's design approach, and we collaborated with many vendor partners for its creation. For instance, *nakashi* (repoussé) work from South India was combined with die-piece work from Ahmedabad. Exquisite textured gold sheet elements were fused with beautiful fine filigree and wire work from Kolkata. We also used a polish to give some of the products an 'otherworldly' patina, that has since become a Tanishq signature. Divyam was launched with Deepika Padukone as the face of the collection.

It was a blockbuster collection, making our competitors scramble unsuccessfully to create lookalikes. Women just loved the jewellery and it created a huge platform for every Diwali: Shubham, Virasat, Padmaavat, Ekatvam, Alekhya, Dharohar. Blockbusters followed every year, every Diwali. This revolution would take Tanishq to the very top of the design/craft/finish table, delivering Rs 25,000 crore of sales of such products since the launch of Divyam, with Divyam itself selling more than Rs 1,000 crore cumulatively.

I have always believed in the power of creative tension: how two collaborating departments can be joined by the larger business goal at one level but can still have their own independent intermediate goals and push each other in pursuit of those – the profit emphasis versus the customer emphasis. Sandeep Kulhalli was focused on profitability, as he should have been. Revathi Kant was focused on customer excitement, as she was supposed to be. How do we maximize on both – these two factors that sometimes appear contradictory? Through pushing each other all the time, through leaders who think differently, through leaders who are themselves different as well!

Anjali Sikka, the designer behind Divyam, was convinced that the most intricate work came only from Jaipur *karigar*s. But Arivazhagan, the head of New Product Introduction, leading the critical Design-Prototype bridge at Tanishq since 2011, wanted a shift, starting with Divyam, for two key reasons: one, to create more capacity for such products; and two, to source them cheaper. Arivazhagan, with Anjali's agreement, decided to shift the development of Divyam out of Jaipur. It was unheard of, but they took the plunge. Our vendor partners in Ahmedabad and Kolkata showed great enthusiasm and exceptional humility, invested substantial time and effort in learning the techniques and delivered the prototypes and bulk to the demanding standards of Anjali.

Sunil Raj is the general manager, Merchandizing, of Tanishq and built the foundations of the merchandizing function over the last fifteen years. 'But it wasn't smooth sailing. We ran into a big issue. The Divyam products were stunning, but the prototypes were all much heavier than what we had asked for.' I also remember the events around this vividly. It was July 2015 or so. We called all the departments into the factory conference room, called the vendor partners as well and said that we needed to retain the exquisiteness of the prototypes, and still bring down the weights of the final production pieces substantially. The designers, the new product development teams, the sourcing teams and the vendors began to work on this. We were doing the prototypes again and concurrently planning for the bulk production. 'Divyam went on to change our Diwali season fortunes forever! The teams were all committed to success and were willing to collaborate to the hilt,' Sunil smiles.

That whole period was a seesaw of regulatory cataclysms. The year 2013 was all about gold import restrictions and GOL abolition, while 2014 brought regulatory controls on public deposits and the GHS. By 2016, we were starting to recover and hoping that was all this all behind us.

Man Proposes, God Disposes

Sometime around 5 p.m. on 8 November 2016, a communication came on various TV channels that the prime minister would address the nation with a special message around 7:30 p.m. I suppose we were all curious about what was going to come, but it turned out to be a huge surprise for all of us and a big shock for some.

Gopalarethinam is another Titan veteran who spent more than thirty years in Titan, mainly in the finance function, across territories and divisions. In 2016, he was heading the commercial function in the Jewellery division. He remembers switching on the TV out of curiosity. By the time the main message from the prime minister had come out, it was around 8 p.m. and time for the Tanishq stores to start closing. He had announced that the Rs 500 and Rs 1,000 currency notes would cease to be legal tender by midnight of that same day – 8 November 2016.

'I remember calling Subbu (Titan's CFO) a few times. But he was probably on his walk and had left his phone. I then called you, Venkat, but we were both unclear about the implications,' Gopal recalls.

In the meantime, our regional retail managers had started reporting a huge rush of customers into our stores, bringing lots of cash and wanting to buy jewellery. Many stores were continuing to deal with those customers and kept the billing going. However, some stores had already shut their systems down (a process called End of Day, EOD, had been completed), but customers were flowing into those stores as well. Confusion prevailed everywhere. Subbu called Gopal soon after that, having come back from his walk. The decision was that we would tell all our stores categorically that the billing would be shut down by midnight and no payments could be made with these notes against any invoice of 9 November or later. Gopal remembers being on the phone through the night on 8 November, rotating his calls across the country, speaking to store managers, regional commercial managers and regional business managers, exhorting all of them to stay firm on this deadline. One of his colleagues, Sulbihar Ali, was his right-hand man that day.

I came to know on the 9th about the chaotic situation in our stores across the country. In the stores that had still been open, there was one kind of bedlam. Customers were crowding the stores to buy jewellery and then standing in the queue for the billing. The billing process became extremely long because of it being 100 per cent cash and with the need to count so many notes for each transaction. At the same time, the store had a midnight deadline to close the billing and was unsure if they could complete the billing in time for every customer. It was a very different problem in the stores which had already done their EOD by 8:30 p.m. The doors of the stores were still open, since the staff were still there, doing their last closure work. Customers thronged in with loads of cash, wanting to buy. But EOD had already been done. If the system was opened again, the date would be 9 November, when the currency notes were invalid! There was intense pressure on us from those customers to sell, and from the stores on Gopal to open the system. But Gopal stood firm and we had to turn away thousands of disappointed customers from those stores.

Gopal remembers Subbu being very worried about all this cash because there was no news about how the banks would deal with these notes and give credit. We were worried that we might be sitting on some junk paper. Fortunately, assurance came from the banks by the end of the 9th on this count. But, the banks said, *please wait, since we cannot collect so much cash so quickly.* The next few days were very complicated and intense for Gopal and his team and the treasury team of Titan Company. Exact store-wise collection details matched to invoices dated 8 November had to be given to ICICI Bank, our partner bank for the Cash Management System. ICICI shared all those details with their cash collection partner company. That company would go to each store with that certified report and take only those many notes of Rs 500 and Rs 1,000 that were in that report. It took nearly a week for that cash to be deposited with ICICI and the credit received in our bank account.

'Amidst all that chaos, two things stand out for me and reinforce everything about Titan. One, no Tanishq store (*of course, no other Titan Brand store as well*) collected a Rs 500 or Rs 1,000 note on 9 November or later. Two, no Tanishq store was sent any notice by the Income Tax department, while there were reports around notices and raids in the media about some jewellery stores,' says Gopal.

After Demonetization

The abolition of these currency notes had its impact on the industry's high-value jewellery since the sales of higher-value products typically had a greater share of cash payment. Sales over the next few months were lower but things started settling thereafter.

The Titan family got a huge jolt in June 2016. Xerxes Desai, founder, maverick, iconoclast, legend and humanitarian passed away in Bengaluru due to a health ailment. He was seventy-nine. I remember breaking down as soon as Bhaskar walked into my room to give me the news. The impact he had on all of us was immeasurable. I did not know it at that time but by throwing me out of his room in 2000 and stopping me from leaving Titan, Xerxes Desai had given me the priceless gift of occupying his chair in a few years to come. His funeral was held in Hosur. It felt like the entire city had turned up for his last journey.

Another significant thing happened in 2016: Titan Company became the majority owner of CaratLane, a digital-first jewellery company started by Mithun Sacheti, a young entrepreneur from a Mumbai-based jewellery family. Mithun was doing seminal work on design and online sales, completely reimagining the jewellery category for young women. We saw a huge opportunity in that venture and invested in CaratLane. In the next few years, CaratLane went from strength to strength, driven by Mithun's, his co-founders' and the CaratLane team's capabilities and passion, the brand support of Tanishq and the network and management support of Titan Company. *(Titan Company became the 100 per cent owner of CaratLane in FY 2023–24.)*

Despite the financial pressures, we stayed on course with our brand strategy – Revitalizing Tradition – and even amplifying it. Two strong examples were the Rivaah film and the *Padmaavat* partnership.

'Bhaskar was convinced that we needed a sub-brand for the wedding business. He kept pushing this idea for almost two years,' smiles Deepika Tewari in recollection. I was also party to this discussion on a few occasions. Bhaskar's view was that the wedding market was so large that it needed focus and a sub-brand was the first step in that direction.

The result was Rivaah, a play around Rivaaz (custom) and Vivaah (wedding) which we launched in 2017.

Deepika had started discussing the Rivaah Brides film with Lowe. The challenge was to make a film that showcased the jewellery of many states and yet had a lot of emotion. RamSam of Lowe recollects settling on the relationship between fathers and daughters as the central idea for the film and deciding to show Marathi, Punjabi, Telugu, Gujarati, Bengali and Tamil wedding situations featuring fathers and daughters. 'I wanted a song that strung all these together,' RamSam smiles. 'We kept asking, what do we say in the song, what do we say in the song – we really struggled for the lyrics and that struggle became the final lyrics! *Kaise kahoon main, samajh na aaye, pyaar diya paglaayi* (how do I say it, it's not clear to me, you gave me love, my little girl) was a deeply melodious and moving song that Hariharan sang with his heart!'

I saw that film in my room in the Titan office in Bengaluru before its release. I asked it to be replayed a couple of times. After it ended, I turned towards the window, away from Deepika and Upasana, Deepika's team member, who were there to show me the film. I heard Deepika whisper to Upasana, 'Let's go!' Deepika later told me, 'Upasana was asking me when we were leaving your room, why was Venkat not giving us his feedback on the film. I told her, 'Upasana, Venkat was crying quietly looking out of the window. That was his feedback!' Even today, many years later, every time I see that film, I tear up. To me, it's the most powerful film ever made for fathers and daughters.

A careful viewing of this film shows the subtle ways in which a new father/daughter relationship is evoked for the viewer, multiple times, a relationship that is only part of the Tanishq world. The film is so much about tradition, showing all the ceremonies, clothes and rituals that are part of our marriages in vivid detail. But it's also so much about its revitalizing, by showing a whole new relationship between daughters and fathers, a relationship that is so free, spontaneous, grown-up, very clearly an aspirational world for the daughters and fathers of our times.

With the many things that we had done over the years: community trousseau, wedding zones in stores and investments in communication, the share of wedding jewellery to total gold jewellery had moved up from 17 per cent in FY 2012 to 21 per cent in FY 2017.

The year 2018 was the year of *Padmaavat*. Queeta Rawat, senior design manager, handled the challenging project. 'Sanjay Leela Bhansali was very difficult to work with. His expectations were sky high, and his deadlines were ridiculous. But the results were completely worth it!' Queeta cancelled her holiday to the US to stay back and take on the *Padmaavat* film project. She recollects sending her mom off alone to the US and then going to make a presentation to Bhansali. The whole project turned out to be super complex. Bhansali's expectations were dynamically changing. As the scope kept increasing, we simply could not budget properly. But despite the murderous deadlines, Queeta was delighted about the opportunity she got. 'Revathi had my back. She said '*Tujhe jaise karna hai, kar!*' (Whatever you need to do, just do it!) That liberated me. Months of work, no days, no nights, no weekends, or holidays, spending all the time with vendors and *karigar*s – I learnt so much about myself, got multiple panic attacks, also got tremendous confidence in myself and learnt so much from Bhansali!' *Padmaavat* was a huge Diwali event of 2018 and further strengthened Tanishq's perception as a jeweller.

The manufacturing transformations accelerated in this period. The operations of Tanishq today are a world apart from where it began in 1994, impressing even those employees who moved out in 2004. Automation is all-pervasive: diamond bagging automation, casting bagging automation, kit marshal automation and warehouse automation. Precision technology is everywhere: AI-controlled Benzinger computer numerical control (CNC) systems for ring making and diamond setting and high-speed machines for manufacturing a variety of gold chains. We have one of the world's largest and best gold refining plants. Even to the most discerning jewellery experts from across the world, the Hosur plant is awe-inspiring in its scale, scope and depth of technology. Of course, the thousands of customers of Tanishq who have visited the plant in the last ten years have been equally impressed. Their photo-op moment is the one where they valiantly try to lift a deceptively small 10-kilogram bar of 24-karat gold!

This kind of backbone is unique in the jewellery industry. No other jewellery retailer is anywhere close on this front. Even those who are showing intentions of investing in manufacturing and vendor development are in the very early stages, and the gap between Tanishq and them will remain for a very long time.

Here are some important questions: *Is your organization the category expert all-round or at least in the most critical parts of your category value chain? How clear are you about those parts? How obsessed are you about building that expertise?*

The GHS enrollments returned in a big way by FY 2017, and the sales growth rate started coming back to double digits. By the end of 2017, we were back to our normal selves, confident enough to announce a 2.5x sales revenue of FY 2018 in FY 2023. Despite the low growth rates of the earlier few years, the market opportunity was still huge, and we were quite convinced that our competitive advantage and execution capabilities remained as strong as ever. Five long-term growth engines have been identified to make this 2.5x happen. The first year of these five years, FY 2019, was quite good. FY 2020 started to look a bit challenging, and the end of Calendar 2019 was further complicated by leadership changes in Titan (I took over as MD on 1 October 2019) which occupied some of us for a while. We were just settling into our new seats and starting to figure out how to get back to our growth trajectory. And then Covid struck.

5

Leader to Legend: 2019–2023

Bhaskar Bhat had been part of what became the Titan Watch project in Tata Press, way back in the early 1980s, so, technically he was the first employee of Titan Watches Limited. He had been there in the project office in the Taj West End Hotel in Bengaluru in the mid 1980s when the small team led by Xerxes Desai had decided in favour of the quartz technology. He had been there on the road through the first few years after Titan's launch, meeting watch dealers and placing the watches in their counters. Over the years, he had been at the front and centre of everything in Titan Company. He took over from Xerxes Desai as the MD on 1 April 2002 and was retiring on 30 September 2019, after seventeen years as the MD. He was (and still is) a legend and everyone's friend – an exquisitely rare combination.

It was his shoes that I stepped into when I became the MD of Titan on 1 October 2019. Of course, it helped that I was also a Titan veteran, having completed twenty-nine years in the company. With my fourteen years in Watches and fifteen years in Jewellery, I knew almost everyone in the company, all the directors on the board, a few senior folks in the Tata group and many others, but Bhaskar was Bhaskar and the expectations from me were daunting. Many of my other senior colleagues were also retiring around the same time. In fact, the current CXO council (MD + the senior CXOs) was getting completely refreshed. As part of our growth strategy for the next many years, we also carved out three new business divisions and got in three CEOs for those. The first few months passed in a daze with most of us in totally new roles.

It was 9 March 2020 and the CXO Council of Titan were all at a meeting with the Risk Management Committee (RMC) of the Titan board at the Taj Vivanta, MG Road, Bengaluru. One of the roles of the RMC was to critically evaluate the Annual Operating Plan from the overall risk perspective before the plan was finally presented to the entire board of Titan in the last week of March. The ultra-positive people that we all were, the early news of COVID-19 had not touched our confidence. Our annual plan as well as the April–June Quarter 1 plan were quite gung-ho, in our usual style. We had identified just a minor niggle to our growth plans, which was our dependence on China for our watch parts.

Ireena Vittal had been an independent director on the board of Titan for many years and was also the RMC chair. 'Global companies and leaders are looking at a 60–70 per cent drop in sales. I feel you are being way too optimistic!' Known for her absolute clarity and total bluntness, this comment from her was par for the course. I bristled at this criticism and defended our stand and offered a response that 'in our view, the Covid risk was not that big,' which was her point in any case!

Within just two weeks after that meeting, the country went into lockdown for six weeks and the first quarter of FY 2021 turned out the way Ireena had predicted it would. I was staring at managing the worst quarter in the history of Titan Company. Fortunately, I had the sense to look at the crisis with a holistic perspective. It was not my failure or our collective failure at Titan. The whole world was in crisis and the only way was up. I spoke widely about the need to remain in the 'eye of the storm' while it raged all around us so that we could do the best we were capable of, without letting the stress affect us. I also knew from experience that the jewellery industry ended up doing well even when people were anxious, and was confident that our recovery from Covid would be quick.

So, in April of 2020, it was all about supporting our employees and partners and their employees, financially and emotionally. It was about reassuring people that there was no need to feel anxious at all, that we would all come out of it soon, and that all of us and our families needed to remain safe. There were many things we did to make our employees and partners relax. Pay cuts were minimal (reversed later in 2020 itself) and limited to managers; there were no retrenchments; all partners were supported with minimum pay for all their employees for a few months; vendor partners were not only paid on time but all the materials they had with them were taken by us and credits created for them as well.

Arun Narayan, VP of Retail, Merchandizing and Marketing of Tanishq, a twenty-seven-year veteran at Titan took on that role on 1 April 2020 from Sandeep Kulhalli. Arun smiles, 'On the first day in my new role, all stores were shut. But I felt rather relaxed since the attention was totally diverted from me. Everyone was seized by the crisis.' Arun recollects deciding not to think of business at all and choosing to focus on the staff, their families and customers. He remembers being on calls with

Titan's field employees, store employees and franchisee partners all the time, telling them *this too shall pass!* He and his team got the store staff to call the customers, to ask about their welfare and offer support.

I remember being on a Zoom chat with ten customers in the middle of June 2020, when about five of them recalled being called by their favourite Tanishq store staff and being checked on. They said they did not remember many companies making such calls without any reference to sales. More than 1 million 'empathy' calls were made during the first lockdown.

'The store staff ran with this idea even more,' recalls Arun. I also remember being told about this. In Pune, for example, the store staff prepared a list of doctors, all of them our customers, with their specializations and contact numbers. When any employee or customer contracted the virus, that list kicked in, helping deliver advice, Remdesivir, hospital admission and even oxygen cylinders during the second wave. The work done by the Rapid Response Team of Titan (RRT) was unbelievable and selfless. RRT had members from Retail Ops, People, Admin and Safety.

The RRT was designed as a three-layer pyramid. At the top of the pyramid were eighteen team leads, each one being responsible for one domain (medicines, hospitalization, testing, Covid-care, etc.). Each team lead was also responsible for twenty section leads at the next level (there were 360 section leads in the mid level of the pyramid: 18 x 20). Each section lead was responsible for twenty employees, the third level in the pyramid. Any employee, anywhere in the country, had to simply reach their section lead with the problem through their WhatsApp group. Depending on the nature of the problem, that section lead would reach out to the team lead who was the national anchor for that domain (say, medicines like Remdesivir). In a two-click process, superfast bridges ended up getting created between the problem and solution for rapid closure.

Ajoy Chawla, CEO of the Jewellery division, remembers being calm about the crisis, even as early as the first week of April 2020. 'Clearly, it was everyone's problem, so there was no point in stressing about it. If we were to direct all our energies on resolving the situation, we could be the fastest to come out of the crisis. On reflection, I feel that I ended up subconsciously transferring this calmness to my team members, to our partners and further onwards. It surely must have helped.'

When a business crisis takes over your organization, what's the natural impulse of the leaders? To become anxious, cut costs and put everyone under severe stress?

All in the name of 'company' and 'shareholder' interest? Or do they have the maturity to realize that it's the people who ultimately create all the value? If they are energized, if they are positive and relaxed, they will take all the challenges as their own and simply go about solving them.

The biggest pressure on me in the last week of March 2020 was regarding cash. We had been a zero-debt company for many years thanks to GOL and GHS, and we were staring at a big debt situation by the end of June 2020. As I was grappling with this challenge in the first week of lockdown, I realized that the solution was hiding in plain sight. We had thousands of crores of gold with us, the most liquid asset in the world! The decision was quite simple. Since the inventory requirements for a low sales quarter were also low, we would melt the jewellery, sell it for cash and achieve a positive cash flow.

Vijay Govindarajan, associate vice president (AVP), Finance, at Titan, headed the commercial function in the Jewellery division from 2019 to 2023. 'It was a very complex task, converting that idea into action,' he says. The Merchandizing department had to identify those pieces which were least required for sales and confirm which stores these pieces were sitting in. We are talking about stores spread across the country. Then we had to get those stores opened during the lockdown with special permission to pick up the pieces. They were then shipped to Hosur for melting, refining and converting to 24-karat gold. This 24-karat gold had to be shipped to Pamp (an approved refinery in Gurgaon) for converting into 'Good Delivery' 24-karat bars. Only such certified bars could be sold in the open market. A lot of departments had to work in a collaborative manner and under such constrained circumstances.

Close to Rs 650 crore of gold bullion was sold between May and June of 2020, and this helped Titan Company tide over a challenging period quite comfortably. Since then, the sale of bullion has become a way to manage inventory and cash flows from time to time and has become an established practice in the company.

Vijesh Rajan became the head of Retail of Tanishq in April 2020. 'My first day in the new role was during the lockdown,' he smiles. 'It was mind-numbing, like being put in a freezer.' He recollects not having a single clue about store protocols and what should be done whenever the stores opened. 'People were dying all around us. We realized that we had to take care of our people who were our truest assets. And, of course, our customers. Thus began the journey of Tanishq's Gold Standard in Safety. Retail Ops, Admin, Safety and the Visual Merchandizing teams were involved in creating the playbook.'

The Tanishq Story

I vividly remember this Gold Standard in Safety in play during 2020 and all through 2021. On a visit to the Tanishq Bilaspur store in October 2021, I was following the franchisee and our team into the store when I was stopped at the doorway by the security guard. I was surprised since I was already wearing a mask. When I pointed to my mask, he said, 'Sir, double mask please.' He was not bothered that I was the special guest for the day, so intent was he on following the standard operating procedure (SOP). I smiled at him through the mask, took the second mask he held out for me, put it on my face and walked into the store.

There were so many things to think about, so many things kept evolving – sanitizers, oximeters, various types of masks to try out, various types of shields as well. The staff used to get headaches wearing the shield, so we had to keep modifying the designs. We had to put up PVC screens in front of cashiers, rostering staff and create buffer teams to intervene when people fell sick. We were so strict with this protocol that the daily gold rate would not flow to a store until the morning safety walk-through video was uploaded and certified by the central team. The store could not do any work on the system without having completed this process. Our customers started noticing this obsessive safety procedure and comparing it with whatever was happening in other places. Vijesh is justifiably proud when he shares, 'That's when we started calling it the Gold Standard in Safety.' The Gold Standard in Safety was a big contributor to increasing customer confidence in shopping and getting them to visit the stores of Tanishq as early as June 2020.

The staff in Tanishq stores wore double masks and a plastic shield for many hours every day and for nearly two years! They had to speak to customers through those two masks and a shield, answering their questions and convincing them about the value of Tanishq. No thanks are enough for this sacrifice, but I keep communicating my gratitude to them even as recently as in December 2023 during my store visits across the country. To recognize their extraordinary effort, we featured a salesperson wearing the double mask and shield, in uniform, on the cover of Titan's FY 2021 Annual Report.

Many people started hearing about our standards through word of mouth. And, because of this, many fence-sitters jumped over to Tanishq for the first time. 'The situation was rapidly transforming from mind-numbing to mind-blowing!' Vijesh smiles.

'Given the situation, I was starting to look at virtual try-on as a big intervention,' Arun recalls. 'I spoke to Mithun (Mithun Sacheti, the founder and MD of CaratLane,

Titan's subsidiary).' Mithun told Arun that virtual try-on was rather clunky, and suggested that he go with live-assisted video calling through WhatsApp. Gnanavel (the head of the Customer Order Department) and his team put together the first live-assisted video calling prototype in Hosur. Then Chitti Babu, head of Store Design and Visual Merchandizing, and his team designed a very practical unit for each store with white and yellow lights (for diamond and gold jewellery, as the case may be) shining on a bust where the salesperson would display one product at a time while talking to the customer on WhatsApp video. Arun had this scaled super fast and Tanishq did Rs 100 crore of sales through this just in August 2020. 'It was unbelievable, how both the staff and our customers adapted to the new world,' he says in disbelief. Necessity is evidently the mother of invention. Despite conversations around video-calling as long back as 2018, we had not even managed reaching sales worth Rs 10 crore in the whole of 2019. And here we had made it to Rs 100 crore in just one month!

The other big achievement of 2020 was bringing substantial predictability to the monthly sales. Over the years, the store staff had used customer information stored in Excel sheets to reach out to them with new product messages and promotional offers, especially on their birthdays and anniversaries. However, this manual process limited the efforts and results. Vijesh and the team realized that they needed to get every store to construct a minimum level of sales from its existing customers and assiduously work towards it, minimizing the dependence on new customers walking in. This framework called the Tanishq Operating Rhythm (TOR) was combined with the database that Tanishq already had through its investment in the Customer 360 (the Customer Relationship Management digital platform), whose use was limited around that time. For this, we needed a shift in mindset from the store staff and the franchisee partners, to get them comfortable with technology. They started with eleven pilot stores first and then eleven cities. The single biggest rationale that they communicated was that we had such a large database, and we knew so much about our customers' preferences and milestone events that we could generate substantial sales by capitalizing on that knowledge. *Which customer liked modern diamond jewellery? Who shopped more during promotions? Whose birthdays/milestone birthdays and anniversaries/milestone anniversaries were falling on which days of each month?* Answers to such questions started flowing every day (and ahead of the milestone events) to each store, and tasks got assigned to individual store staff based on their connections with each customer (each customer was tagged to an individual salesperson through the earlier purchase). Potentially this meant thousands of salespersons communicating with tens of thousands of customers every day.

During the pandemic, the need for sales was also very high. Many stores were looking for new ideas and programmes that would help them. And Vijesh and the team found surprising early adopters from small towns as well – which gave them excellent results. A combination of emails, WhatsApp messages and 'reels' topped up by personal calls from the sales staff was used. The cause-and-effect news spread very fast and within a short time, the whole network had gone digital.

Over the next few years, the TOR would hum efficiently, repeat customer share (the effect of TOR) would cruise at a healthy 55 per cent.

The Ekatvam controversy was easily the most stressful period in my career. Ekatvam was the 2020 Diwali collection that followed in the tradition of Divyam, Shubham and Padmaavat. To launch this collection, the brand team and the creative agency had come up with an unusual setting. It was a Muslim household, with a Hindu daughter-in-law. The daughter-in-law was pregnant and the entire film was about the celebration of her baby shower function, around which the Ekatvam jewellery collection was showcased. The protagonists were the Hindu daughter-in-law, her Muslim mother-in-law and some guests. Many people took objection to the film as soon as it was released. It received backlash and trolling on social media, with some people calling it 'anti-Hindu' and others alleging that it promoted 'love jihad'. It soon became the biggest controversy in the whole country. Crowds picketed some of the Tanishq stores, threatening violent action. There was an increasing demand for that film to be pulled down and for Tanishq to apologize. But many others rose to the support of Tanishq, saying there was nothing objectionable in the film at all as it was encouraging harmony and Tanishq should stay the course, continue running the film and not apologize. Ranjani Krishnaswamy, general manager, Marketing, of Tanishq between 2019 and 2023 remembers one side heckling us – '*How dare you do this, pull it down!*', and the other side putting pressure on us – '*Don't you dare withdraw the film! Show your spine!*' In the end, the decision came easily to us. We did not want tensions around any Tanishq store, and we certainly did not want to put any of our colleagues at risk. It had become a matter of principle to everyone outside the company. To us, it was just an ad that we had got wrong, without intending to. It was pointless standing firm on a 'principle' that was not even there to start with. So, we pulled it down. The most stinging rebuke that came my way about that decision was from a friend of Mr Desai, and it was shared with me by an ex-colleague. 'If Xerxes had been the MD, the film would not have been withdrawn!' I took the rebuke and went on with life.

Heading South

Sharad, a thirty-year Titan veteran who is currently the AVP of Gold Jewellery Manufacturing and Sourcing in the Jewellery division, took on the role of the regional business head, South, in June 2019. Among the many things he had done in Titan, Sharad had also been the head of Retail and Marketing for the Gold Plus brand, which had been created for small-town India in 2005. Given that experience, he was quite familiar with the relatively weaker performance of Tanishq in Tamil Nadu. This weak performance was on account of two factors. One, Tamil Nadu was dominated by a few jewellers who had built a huge franchise over decades and had customers coming to their Chennai stores from all over the state. They were not easy to displace. Two, historically, Tanishq had used versions of its national programmes and policies in Tamil Nadu, without an effective use of the relevant customer insights and idiom. This is what Sharad had wanted to change.

The first big project he started was Sigaram (Tamil for peak). He knew that many things had been attempted in the past to grow market share in Tamil Nadu, but with no noticeable success. So, there was scepticism around it. Fortunately, new people were taking up leadership roles and had a natural tendency to try new things. The market share of Tanishq in every big city of Tamil Nadu was in the low single digits. Sharad and the team started with an audacious goal of 10 per cent plus market share. Everyone got excited. The team concluded that they needed to do many big things in an integrated manner. The gold rates had to be competitive. The gold exchange policy had to become attractive. All the product gaps had to be filled systematically and quickly. The existing stores needed transformation. Expansion into new towns needed ratcheting up. Tanishq needed an aspirational brand face (Nayanthara, a leading and respected actor was signed up). A powerful on-ground programme to connect with customers (*pudhumai penn*, Tamil for progressive woman, was created to honour women achievers in different fields). 'Three years of seamless working between the region and the corporate team helped us do everything that we had planned to do and achieve the 10 per cent plus market share. It was heady feeling,' Sharad smiles.

The Sigaram team won the Dream Team Award, which is Titan's highest award for teamwork.

From 2020 to 2023, Tanishq, Mia and Zoya set had a scorching pace of growth. The established engines of growth were given new impetus and new audacity. Some were reimagined, while some were created afresh, like the Digital Leap Forward. The Digital Leap Forward was a combination of a huge Omni-Channel emphasis, a significant thrust behind Endless Aisle (a customer in a particular store having the digital visibility to the jewellery stock in the entire country and ordering a piece through that app to be delivered to her in that store a few days later) and a very respectable pure online sale through the Tanishq website. The sales generated through this thrust would cross 10 per cent of total sales by FY 2023. A Special 26 (Special Chhabbees) target for FY 2022 was taken. It echoed the popular Akshay Kumar movie, ironically set around a jewellery scam. Then there was a Special 36 (Special Chhathees) for FY 2023. These represented Rs 26,000 crore and Rs 36,000 crore in sales revenue in FY 2022 and FY 2023 (in uniform consumer price terms). FY 2023 was the biggest blockbuster year in the history of Tanishq, with a 37 per cent growth over

FY 2022 and the UCP (Uniform Consumer Price) sales of the Jewellery division crossing Rs 34,000 crore, just short of the fifth-year target set in the 2018 Five-Year Plan. Profits surged to cross Rs 4,363 crore, the highest ever by a substantial margin.

The Future of Tanishq

'What are your dreams for Tanishq now?' I ask Ajoy Chawla, the CEO of the Jewellery division.

'There are a few that I am consumed by,' replies Ajoy. 'Every woman in India should want to own a Tanishq. Every bride should say that she wanted a Tanishq, even if she did not get one. The aspiration for Tanishq should be that powerful. Every woman should feel that only Tanishq understands her. Tanishq should become the standard for exquisite jewellery for weddings and special occasions, combining design, rare gems and exceptional craftsmanship. Tanishq should be the leader in every city we operate in. I feel there's so much we can do on the sustainability front. While we are doing quite well on the use of recycled gold (around 35 per cent in 2023), can we dream of 100 per cent?'

'I dream of Tanishq being present across twenty-five/thirty cities in the world. Maybe starting with the Indian diaspora, but not restricted to it.'

In our 2019 Business Associate Meet in Istanbul, when I was the CEO of the Jewellery division, I outlined my dream for Tanishq. I had titled it *LTL – Leader to Legend*. The dreams were similar.

Even as we are dreaming aloud, the challenges are also jumping out.

In the last five years, the action in the jewellery market has intensified significantly. Many national, regional and city-level players have realized the importance of designed collections, brand ambassadors, big marketing budgets, heightened store experiences and customer relationships. These players are attracting money as well as talent. While this has accelerated the formalization of the category, it is also providing customers with multiple choices. Tanishq will need to work harder to keep the differentiation gap. Also, increasing scale puts tremendous pressure on execution and on keeping the standards even at today's level. So, competitive intensity and execution excellence are two challenges.

Another challenge is the changing profile of the Indian jewellery customer. The young woman of today has a mind of her own. For her, jewellery is more a self-expression, an accessory, an emotional symbol than a mark of ethnic identity or a store of value. The traditional codes that the Indian jewellery brands represent can start becoming dated in just one decade. So, Tanishq needs to reinvent itself and put much more fuel behind Zoya, Mia and CaratLane, the other brands in the jewellery portfolio.

Tanishq does have some things to watch out for. But, as we always say in Titan, there's so much excitement on our plate!

'What's the *international* dream for Tanishq,' I ask Kuruvilla Markose, the CEO of Titan's International Business Division, the go-to-market arm that was created in 2019 to take Titan global. Kuruvilla is known to everyone as Diny.

'Tanishq should become a global brand, loved by the Indian diaspora, of course, but also reaching into global audiences that love to immerse themselves in other cultures. By the time I moved into my role, the Indian diaspora was jumping out as a huge opportunity for Tanishq,' replies Diny, famous in Titan for his idealism and ability to synthesize multiple ideas into a single, cohesive thought.

Diny and the team partnered with McKinsey to do a systematic assessment of the international opportunity. This work was completed in the second half of 2018. McKinsey recommended Titan to prioritize the West Asian countries, starting with the UAE, over the US, on account of the Indian diaspora market being much larger there than the one in the US. So, the team went about setting up the first Tanishq store in Meena Bazaar, Dubai. Diny continues, 'We opened the Meena Bazaar store in Dubai on 25 October 2020, with Covid raging all around us. Considering Tanishq was going international again after a decade, it was a bit of a baby step, a single-shutter store sandwiched between a double-shutter store of Malabar and Damas,' he chuckles.

'What was the initial response, Diny?' I ask.

'We could not believe that there was so much latent demand for Tanishq,' Diny smiles. 'We were pleasantly surprised. Almost every customer told us, what took you so long to come? You should have been here five years back!'

I should take the blame for that long delay. You may remember from an earlier chapter that we had opened two Tanishq stores in the US in 2007, targeting mainstream American women. We ended up shutting them down in less than two years after realizing that it was going to be a long haul to make them work. Also, the financial crisis of 2008 reduced whatever appetite for risk we had for such a venture. All in all, that launch was considered a failure, perhaps a misjudgment as well. You may also remember that the Tanishq brand had grown 16x between 2005 and 2013. It was during that scorching pace of domestic growth that the international 'misadventure' happened. Given the huge sales growth that we were seeing in India for a long time to come, I had convinced myself that focusing only on India was the best use of resources and management time, especially when growth was so high and appeared relatively easy. I had even developed a convincing argument against going outside India. 'While India is just one nation, it is many economies put together, so why do we need to go to other countries?' which sounded quite smart to me and perhaps ended up convincing others as well.

Of course, between 2013 and 2016, we had multiple domestic regulatory challenges that kept us busy. But the CAD crisis and the 80/20 rule exposed our domestic-dependence underbelly. We realized that we needed a thriving international business. It took us a couple more years after that to start putting a new organization in place that was dedicated to taking Tanishq, and the rest of Titan, global. Headed by a CEO who reported to the MD, getting the necessary resources, freedom and sponsorship, which was what Diny was doing.

During these many years, had I made a few trips to West Asia and the US, had I immersed myself in the jewellery markets there and met Indian customers to understand their needs, I am certain that the opportunity would have jumped out and we would have set up our stores earlier. But I did not do that on account of my conviction about India and the consequent dismissal of the opportunity outside. I had become a frog in the well, if you will.

Having a full-time CEO for international business was a transformational decision. Diny was dreaming all the time about international expansion. 'While our initial decision was to go to the US *after a couple of years*, over two visits we changed our decision and decided to open stores in the US as well.'

Non-Resident Indians/People of Indian Origin (NRI/PIO) in the US had become well-to-do, particularly in the last ten years. They had also become quite confident and expressive about their ethnicity. The Indian community in the US had an average income of USD 100,000 compared to USD 60,000 average for the whole of the US. And they were also celebrating marriages and festivals in a big way and wearing their Indianness on their sleeve. Some of them were buying Tanishq on their visits to India, of course, but the local opportunity in the US was manifold. And we needed partners for that.

Our Tanishq franchisee in Jalandhar, Mr Bains, had his daughter and son-in-law living in New Jersey. He had been convinced about the Tanishq opportunity in the US for quite a long time and he offered to become our first franchisee in the US and that's how the US operations began.

I will talk about the partnership philosophies of Titan Company later in the book, but without a doubt, the franchisee partners of Tanishq have played a crucial role in its success in India and were destined to play that role outside India as well. In the big dream that Diny and the team are shaping for Tanishq outside India – forty stores in multiple cities across continents – the India franchisees are partnering with us in many places and connecting us with their friends in other places.

'I had not known Azmat before,' smiles Diny, referring to Azmat Siddiqui, the Tanishq franchisee who runs the Allahabad and Moradabad stores of Tanishq. 'Azmat met me and said that he would like to set up the Houston store of Tanishq for his son. I said, "Yeah let's talk about it. Which college does your son go to?" Azmat then told me that his son was three years old!' cracks up Diny. The Houston store opened in November 2023.

Balaji Natarajan, currently an independent store design consultant, designed the US stores of Tanishq, and also headed Store Design and Visual Merchandizing for Tanishq for about ten years, starting around 2001. 'It was hugely exciting and equally challenging, designing the first

US store and then executing it with American partners and civil contractors,' he recollects, talking about the New Jersey store. We wanted to create a store which was exclusively a Tanishq store, but which also stood out in a more sophisticated retail environment like the US. Balaji and the team also emphasized on sustainable materials for the packaging and product presentations. He recalls that the American partners were very impressed with the team's sensitivity about such matters. 'The crowning glory was when a leading store design magazine in the US gave us an Award of Merit for this first store,' says a delighted Balaji.

I had gone for the inauguration of this New Jersey store in January 2023. The special guests were a US senator and congressman, friends of our franchisee (our Jalandhar franchisee's son-in-law). When it was my turn to speak, I couldn't resist the chance to throw a challenge at the Americans. 'The founder of our company and the man who visualized Tanishq, Xerxes Desai, had a dream to create the Tiffany of the East. Today, Tanishq has dropped anchor here in New Jersey, just across the Hudson River from Tiffany. Yesterday, I was on Fifth Avenue (in New York City) and very close to the Tiffany store (the iconic flagship store of Tiffany). I could hear the tremors from that building. Those folks are surely getting nervous.' The senator and congressman laugh at this. But I add for serious measure, 'The Titan Company, of which Tanishq is a part, is today the most valuable jewellery company in the world.' This gets a bigger applause from the crowd, which is mostly Indian!

The sales response from the American stores (in Edison, New Jersey; Houston, Texas; and Dallas, Texas, as I write this) was pleasantly surprising. But what gladdens our hearts equally is the significant change in the industry that we have brought into the US – the design differentiation, the craftsmanship and quality of our product finish, the transparency in diamond pricing, the superlative store experience and the international exchange policy. People are seeing this as a breath of fresh air. It's been much the same in the Middle East and Singapore as well. Other countries in the Middle East are on the cards; other cities in the US are on the way; Canada and the UK beckon while Australia is raising its hand as well.

'What more?' I ask Diny. 'The Indian diaspora is our foundation, of course. But the opportunity is much wider. The Emiratis, Filipinos and the Jordanians in the UAE, and the Asians and Hispanics in the US as well. And why not the Caucasians and African Americans?'

As we take Tanishq outside Indian market localities and into mainstream shopping areas in the US and elsewhere, these opportunities will become concrete and real. The photo of our first Congolese customer within the first week of our Houston store opening confirms this hypothesis. My meetings in Houston and Dallas with Americans of various hues and vintages strengthen my belief in this exciting and large opportunity.

Tanishq can become the largest and most desired jewellery brand in the world. All it needs is one decade. Perhaps Xerxes Desai had thought all this through. Perhaps the whole 22-karat detour in 1997 was merely a roundabout way to take Tanishq to where he wanted it to be from inception.

By setting up stores in the US, Tanishq has brought the '*jung*' to the '*maidan*' if you will! (brought the battle to the amphitheatre). Ironically, the kind of jewellery we are now starting to make for the US, for Indians and Americans alike, is a bit like the 18-karat diamond jewellery that we struggled to sell in India in 1996.

Jai Hind!

Part 2

The Foundations

What makes a company successful?

Why has Tanishq managed to grow higher over the years? Its success lies in several key principles, management approaches and philosophies that any individual can learn from.

How much importance does an organization give to innovation?

How much focus is given to breakthrough innovation?

How much effort is put into involving every single employee in continuous improvement?

How institutionalized is the innovation culture?

Is the customer obsession of the company mere party line? Or is it an assimilated philosophy and practice – a living, breathing tenet that drives everything that the organization does?

How does an organization create and sustain limitless love and affection from its customers?

How naturally does stakeholder capitalism come to the leaders in the organization?

Are vendors and franchisees true partners in a fulfilling, magical common journey or are they mere tools that are tolerated till they are useful?

How does the organization think and feel about its employees? Are they just factors of production or sales? Or are they members of a large family that looks out for each other, caring and sharing for each other, without compromising the highest standards of performance that they have set out for themselves?

How much time do leaders spend on the ground, particularly in the front? How infallible do they consider themselves? How open are they to criticism? How much do they put themselves in the firing line?

These questions become critical in the understanding of the Tanishq journey and success.

The next set of chapters are about stories around those questions.

1

Innovation

How much importance does your organization give to innovation? How much focus is given to breakthrough innovation? How much effort is put into involving every single employee in the subject of continuous improvement? How institutionalized is the innovation culture?

How do we create an environment that enables *breakthrough* innovation?

Necessity is the mother of invention. We have all heard this innumerable times in our lives. Sometimes, we have our backs to the wall. The way out is not clear. We need to rack our brains. Or there are times when our leader has thrown us a hairy, audacious goal, without any suggestion about how we will get there. Both represent tasks that need breakthrough innovation.

One big challenge that Jacob and the team were battling in the early 2000s was the high cost of manufacturing and sourcing.

LRN had joined Tanishq in 2003 as the head of manufacturing, coming off many years in automobile manufacturing. He recollects being in a Titan board meeting a few weeks after joining and a Titan director asking Jacob, 'Have you decided on the date of closure of the jewellery manufacturing plant?' LRN smiles. 'Titan was my twelfth job, and I was starting to wonder – was my thirteenth job around the corner?' LRN's worry did not materialize, and he went on to work in Titan for the next twelve years, till his retirement, establishing formal processes for innovation. In the early 2000s, the jewellery plant was predominantly making 18-karat diamond jewellery. The costs were double of what the same jewellery could have been outsourced for. The setting of the diamonds in the jewellery items required considerable skill and was contributing to the high overall cost. 'I called my team members and said we need a 200 per cent increase in productivity!' LRN chuckles at his own audacity. Imagine the situation – the team members of LRN have by now spent many years in the manufacturing of jewellery while he himself has no experience in jewellery manufacture, having spent the last few years in automobile manufacturing. Sure, he is the boss now, but he has just joined the company. What would he know?

But they all have had their backs to the wall for many years. It is in the last three years that the division has finally turned around. Jacob has got the board to believe in the business opportunity. But manufacturing is still a high-cost operation, and they are painfully aware that they need to bring down the cost. That pressure-cooker situation is ideal for opening everyone to a new leader and for the breakthrough innovation that he is pushing for.

The key operation in the diamond jewellery manufacturing was the setting of stones. It was a very skilled operation. Each setter could set only 100 stones per day. If that could change dramatically, the total manufacturing cost could come down significantly.

B. Manimaran, a Titan jewellery veteran who was put in that pressure-cooker situation in 2003 and is now the divisional manager for Diamond Jewellery Responsible Sourcing, shares with a smile, 'It required out-of-the-box thinking. I called two of my teammates, young guys with a gung-ho attitude, and told them that we should come up with a process through which even a trainee could set 1,000 stones per day, just after one day's training.' This 'impossible' goal excited those two teammates. After a few days, they came back with the idea that resulted in 'wax-setting', where the diamonds were set in the wax replica itself (a stage earlier to when the actual jewellery piece in gold was cast). This took up the productivity to 225 stones per day.

But that was not good enough. The team thought about it a lot more and went further back in the process and tried setting the stones in the rubber mould itself (before the wax replica was even cast). This took up the productivity to 1,000 stones per day! Long story short, the more upstream they went, the less skill was required to set the stones, given the nature of the setting requirements and, thus, higher was the productivity. 'This mould-setting innovation won us the first prize in Tata Innovista (the Tata Group Innovation forum)! We got a patent for it as well,' says Manimaran.

This innovation had a cascading effect on the ISCM team of Titan's Jewellery division to initiate many innovation projects across the board. People started challenging the 'status quo' in their workplaces. Eventually, this led to the creation of a forum called the Innovation School of Management, through which employees were trained on structured innovation processes for quantum leap innovation projects. The mould-setting innovation and a few other things that were done in the early 2000s (covered in Chapter 3 of Part 1) significantly increased the efficiency of the manufacturing and sourcing operations and brought the 'ISCM' back into the reckoning. The challenging circumstances helped, of course, but it required leaders to declare lofty goals and galvanize the talent in pursuit of those.

Pressure-cooker situations do help!

Beate Steinfeld joined us in 2011 to head product innovation in Jewellery. She was a trained German goldsmith and brought with her a deep understanding of jewellery craft and engineering and the well-known German quality of high standards and blunt speaking. 'Our earlier attempts at product innovation were not intense, nor integrated. Then we said let's bring everyone under one roof: product designers, CAD designers, stone setters, all experts.' I remember Beate reaching out to me for enabling this. We put all those experts together in an inspiring environment, which was the tree-shaped Innovation Centre in our Hosur plant. We also gave them less time to innovate – just two weeks! The goal was to identify new ways of illusion setting, a way to put together many small diamonds to mimic the look of a large diamond, a value-for-money solution. Beate smiles in recollection, 'The teams came up with more than forty options. One of them was a patent-winning setting, Maya.'

Sometimes a made-up pressure-cooker situation also helps!

Sanjay Ranawade is the chief manufacturing officer of the Jewellery division and has been driving the manufacturing and sourcing transformation since 2012. 'The HRW (Human Rights Watch, an international NGO) article shook us quite a lot.' He is referring to a 2018 report by HRW which rated the practices of Tanishq as very weak, mostly based on the opacity related to the upstream operations in gold and diamond mines. I vividly remember the day the report came out. We were jolted, embarrassed and angry. We felt that HRW had given too much weight to things beyond our control (gold and diamond mining) and not given enough credit to everything we were doing (manufacturing transformation at vendor units). But, despite the disappointment and disagreement, that report impelled us to look at other parts of the supply chain and spot the improvement potential. The result of that introspection was the Titan Supplier Engagement Protocol (TSEP). TSEP is a programme that focuses on diamond manufacturing and the small units in Surat and Bhavnagar which manufacture the millions of small diamonds used by Tanishq.

India is the global hub of the diamond cutting and polishing industry. The diamantaires, partners of mining companies like De Beers and Al Rosa, have set up advanced manufacturing centres for cutting and polishing the 'rough' diamonds into 'polished' diamonds. However, the very small diamonds could not afford large modern setups and were made in dozens of small units in towns like Bhavnagar. 'TSEP took us deep into the diamond manufacturing territory, got the diamantaires to look within their ecosystem and help upgrade these smaller diamond manufacturing units,' the satisfaction is evident in Sanjay's voice.

As you can see, a big external setback helps!

As leaders, do we let the circumstances overwhelm us, intimidate us into inaction and become stoic or even defensive about the problem? Or do we convert the challenge into an improvement opportunity like the TSEP?

An expression comes to mind: *don't get mad; get even.*

When a storm is raging around us, do we just hunker down and wait for it to pass (in a real storm, that may be the best approach) or do we try and stay inside the 'eye of the storm' and observe the storm dispassionately? The eye of the storm helps us to stay 'outside' the problem and articulate things like 'why can't the output go up by 200 per cent?' or 'we need the factory layout change in just one week!' The results are new pathways that help the organization to shift orbits.

Apart from such a cultural approach that we can build in the organization, what also helps is if the organization has a variety of personalities, each of whom thinks very differently. 'One of the best things about Tanishq was the ability to not just allow contradictions to exist, but also to nurture them. Some of us were very different personalities, but we thrived in Tanishq,' smiles Niraj Bhakare, now the regional business head of Titan Company, who spent nearly sixteen years in Tanishq before taking up this across-company role in 2019. And, as leaders, how do we create our teams? How much emphasis do we put on gathering very different personalities around us, as opposed to accumulating many people 'like' ourselves? Is comfort what we are looking for or is it creativity, innovation and breakthrough thinking? It's something to think about.

Through This Door Pass Ordinary People Who Do Extraordinary Things.

This was the sign on the doorway to the fifth floor in Titan's Bengaluru HQ in the early 2000s, the floor in which Jacob and his Tanishq team used to sit. I was in the Watches division at that time, and I used to marvel at the power and beauty of this phrase. It was a homage to the power and ability within each one of us. If only someone were to empower each one of us completely, what could we end up achieving!

Mark Twain famously said, 'I have never let my schooling interfere with my education'. It's a powerful perspective around our tendency to assume that those who have been to the 'right' school and gotten the 'right' degree always know better. Without taking anything away from 'schooling' and its benefits, wouldn't we all be much better off if we involve everyone around us in making improvements in everything we do? For any organization to be successful, you need many experts. Those experts need to be exceptionally good at what they do, not necessarily good at speaking in English. If you stay firm in this belief and emphasize the role of capability over English communication, then the organization will create cutting-edge products, services and processes. Of course, you need a certain number of managers who need communication skills as well, on top of their capabilities, and that's often in external-facing departments. But, remember, communication skills are not everything; capabilities come first!

Saravanan comes from a very small village called Ponnamaravathi, in Tamil Nadu. He joined Titan straight from school and got into jewellery manufacture: master making, rubber-cutting and quality control. He told me that he used to paint a lot even when he was a kid. That interest and that skill led him to design jewellery. He is now the senior design manager in Tanishq, with many successful collections to his credit. 'Elizabeth (Elizabeth Mathan, the design head in the early 2000s) moved me into Design twenty years back; taught me, encouraged me and told me that my talent and skill were what mattered, *not my ability to speak or present in English*,' Saravanan smiles in recollection.

I remember attending an Innovation Exhibition of Titan's engineering subsidiary which makes parts for aircraft engines sometime in 2018. I was at a stall that showcased a very complex part that they had machined through an innovative approach. The young employee was starting to present to me. He appeared nervous. He started talking and then fumbled a little. Then he stopped and asked me, 'Can I speak in Tamil, sir?' I said, 'Of course'. In a moment, he was transformed. For the next 10 minutes, he just went on and on, speaking so passionately and cogently about this complex engineering problem that he had solved. All in colloquial Tamil.

Do German engineers speak English? Or the Chinese? Or even the Japanese? So much talent and expertise sit in our country but are often circumscribed by the expectations of the world around them to speak in English!

Kaizen and the Art of Improvement

In almost every business environment, there are so many opportunities to make improvements all around. But those opportunities remain unrealized because the people at large are not given an environment or encouragement to do so. The Kaizen programme at Titan has helped all the employees to look around where they work, identify problems or opportunities and create processes to deal with them quite efficiently. This boosts employee engagement and fulfilment with much more organizational effectiveness.

I was at a Kaizen Mela (a fair that we had established in 2008 for showcasing powerful examples of Kaizen – a Japanese approach meaning continuous improvement) in Pune, held in a large hall in a hotel. Afsana Patel, a sales officer in the Tanishq Bund Garden store in Pune was sharing with us her journey in solving a time-consuming operational problem: 'Sir, we have 170 locks in the showroom and every morning we have to match 170 keys to those locks. It was so frustrating.' The words tumble out of Afsana in a torrent. Over the next few minutes, I came to know how much time was wasted every morning in this matching exercise, sometimes even in front of customers. So, one day, Afsana and her colleagues sat down, thought about the problem and went about fixing it. Since the jewellery counters came in various shapes, they had key chains designed in square, oval and round shapes. Then they added a visual of a diamond or gold jewellery piece on them to assign them properly. On top of that, they fixed counter numbers within those categories and put those numbers on the key chains as well. The time for this operation was cut down by half. 'It became so easy!' Afsana shared. The relief as well as pride were palpable in her voice. We moved down the hall, going from stall to stall. Each one had a team standing in it, with a problem they faced in their store, their diagnosis of that problem, their solution for it and the concrete results. The passion, clarity, articulation, conviction and pride – they were all the same at every stall.

Kaizen focuses on eliminating waste, improving productivity and achieving sustained continual improvement in targeted activities and processes of an organization. The famous lean manufacturing system of Japan is founded on the idea of Kaizen or continual improvement.

'I really did not believe in the concepts of lean manufacturing,' Saumen Bhaumik shares with a certain wistfulness. He recollects Somaiya (the consultant at the jewellery factory) being after him to clean the toilets as a symbolic demonstration of service and him being dead against it. But Somaiya was not giving up and kept at Saumen. Saumen remembers smoking two cigarettes in succession one day, pumping himself up and going to the dirtiest toilet in the factory. It took him forty-five minutes to get it into an acceptable state. But as the stains started disappearing from the water closet, Saumen remembers something powerful starting to happen within him. 'That was the crumbling of my ego and my introduction to Lean. Over the next few years, I became a full believer in Lean and wanted to apply it in Retail when I was transferred to lead it.' At the centre of Lean is the elimination of waste – of material, effort and time. And, in the context of retail, waste that the customer will not pay for. The elimination of all those wasteful things will get everyone in the store to give their undivided attention to every customer. The Kaizen programme in retail was to try and eliminate waste and simplify everything. At the centre of Kaizen is the idea that each one of us is gifted enough to contribute to making things around us better. A truly liberating idea!

Srinivasan, who used to work as a sales officer in a Tanishq store a decade back, is now a manager in the commercial department of the Jewellery division. From its inception, Tanishq has been exchanging other jewellers' products. Srinivasan shares, 'In those days, many customers used to ask questions about the Tanishq gold rate being higher, and we had challenges in dealing with their queries.' It struck him that they could compile all the exchange transactions of the previous day (customers exchanging their old non-Tanishq jewellery), calculate the average purity and display that along with that day's gold rate of Tanishq. For instance: 18 April Tanishq Gold Rate: Rs 2,430/gram for 22 karat; 17 April Exchange Purity: 19.6 karat. The difference in purity was 2.4 karat, which was more than 10 per cent (2.4 karat/22 karat). This meant that the Tanishq gold rate premium of 4 per cent (for instance) could be presented with this perspective and justified more concretely. This helped the store staff to talk about our gold rate with confidence.

During Covid-19, we took the Kaizen programme national and digital. The earlier format was regional and physical and came with obvious constraints. Now it's transformed. More than 200 shortlisted teams across businesses and regions post their entries on a digital platform, open to all employees of Titan Company. An Eyecare division employee in Chennai can examine a Kaizen created by another Eyecare employee in Delhi NCR and adopt it straight away. A Jewellery employee can examine a Kaizen of a Watches employee and use it if relevant. Scaling and cross-pollination can be extremely easy and fast. The final competition comes down to some thirty-odd teams and happens physically in Bengaluru/Hosur, live-streamed to the whole country. The National Digital Kaizen Mela Retail and Kaizen Mela Manufacturing/Fulfilment are held in alternate years, creating a huge pool of incremental innovation, and substantially energizing employees at the same time. The winning entries are taken up by the businesses or functions for scaling.

Alagappan heads customer service for Tanishq today and was the co-conspirator of Saumen in the Kaizen journey. 'The Kanban (Visual Display system, another Japanese concept) journey was also unbelievable!' Alagappan is unable to contain his excitement and the words are tumbling out nonstop.

Let me illustrate the Kanban system using jewellery pieces and their packaging boxes. Given the variety of jewellery items, there may be forty types of packaging items, let's say five different boxes of five necklace types, three boxes for three bangle types and so on. Now, the jewellery items are shipped separately to the store and not in their packaging boxes, which are sent separately. This is done principally to avoid the possible damages in shipping. This means that the planning of the quantities for these would be unsynchronized. Hence, you could suddenly discover that you have run out of a box for a particular 'choker' necklace that the store has just billed. The Kanban system solves this challenge visually. Long story short, a visual display is created in the packaging storage area which helps the person responsible for the packaging material in the store to assess the stock level of each packaging type, become aware that it is time to order that item and order the right quantity immediately. This 'manual' system helps synchronize, in this case, the product and its packaging. Can you imagine the pantry lady using the Kanban system for her stock of coffee powder, just so that she can request the purchase of the powder at the right time, instead of creating some last-minute tension? We were teaching the sales staff the Kanban process for packing material and the housekeeping lady was learning Kanban on the go and applying those principles to her situation! Over the years I have met security guards, housekeeping ladies and valets who have created their kaizens in their workspaces to simplify things around them and make their work easier. The passion and joy that they conveyed while relating their stories are impossible to share and can only be experienced. But what has always been clear is that, by empowering people and encouraging every person to look around them and solve their problems, we ended up creating magic!

2

Customer Obsession

Is the customer obsession of the company mere party line? Or is it an assimilated philosophy and practice – a living, breathing tenet that drives everything that the organization does? How does an organization create and sustain limitless love and affection from its customers?

'It does not matter if the customer walks out of the store empty-handed. But she must walk out with a smile on her face, a smile in her eyes, a smile in her heart.' It has become a rote speech for me in English, Hindi and Tamil. I say it every day, sometimes four or five times a day. I have relayed it to all the store staff, over weeks, months and years.

The journey began sometime in 2007 when Bhaskar requested Prof. Das Narayandas of Harvard Business

School to conduct a workshop for Titan managers on customer experience and delight. Das, a professor of marketing at Harvard, and an independent director of Titan later for many years, engaged us with his wicked style, with global examples of companies that are the gold standard in customer understanding and experience. He ended up lighting a spark in many of us. We decided to start a programme to understand our customers comprehensively and deeply and delight them in a sustained way to build loyalty and advocacy. This customer-focused approach was titled 'Creating Fans for Life' – a term coined by Aanchal Jain, a colleague.

Bidyut Nath joined Tanishq in 2007 to set up the customer loyalty programme, which was named Anuttara. Bidyut recalls, 'The store managers and the senior staff were quite sceptical about an organized loyalty programme that was built on customer data. They said, "We know our customers personally and all their information is in our diaries. Customers won't want their purchase details to be known or analysed."' I also remember that there was a big pushback from the store staff. But we were convinced that we needed to understand customers deeply. Apart from their actual purchases, we also needed to know the special occasions in their lives, details about their family, their hobbies and preferences. This approach was not anything new, but we wanted to integrate it into the lives of the sales staff so that customer understanding could lead to sales impact and advocacy in a very visible way. Bidyut adds, 'That's why the Loyalty responsibility was sitting under Retail in Tanishq, while in most companies it was part of the Marketing function.'

How deep is our understanding of our customers outside the sales information? Even if all we know is the sales data, how much have we invested in tools to understand that information? *This lady seems to buy only around festivals, or she seems to be keen on promotions or new products seem to be her interest.* If we knew any of this or all of this, we could communicate with her at the right time with the right messages. But there is a huge power sitting outside the sales information as well. When you know personal things about your customers, magic can happen. When we started celebrating the customers' birthdays at their homes, we took customer delight to another level. No company was sending a salesperson home with a cake to celebrate the customer's birthday. It created an unbelievable impact. Bidyut remembers a salesperson talking about a lady customer crying at home on her birthday, telling the salesperson that her children who lived abroad had forgotten to wish her that day while Tanishq had made the effort! The birthday celebrations would also sometimes happen in the store in front of many other customers to take the delight quotient to greater heights. I was a personal witness to this approach as recently as in October 2022, when I happened to be in Vadodara on my birthday. I was at the Tanishq store at around 6 p.m. The word somehow got to the store staff that it was my birthday (with customers, entering their mobile numbers would have triggered that alert). The franchisee partner, Nirav Kothari, arranged a cake at short notice for me to cut in front of many customers who were watching this event with so much shared joy. I was over the moon!

Starting in 2007, we did many things from a systemic point of view to make all these happen. We appointed customer experience executives (as part of Bidyut's team) in every region, whose job was only focusing on customer experience. We recommended that all the area and regional managers meet customers frequently. All our monthly review meetings started with customer metrics before we reviewed sales metrics. We started recognizing salespeople in public forums for customer delight stories and gave attractive rewards for those, including trips to the head office and factories.

Anirban Banerjee spent more than fifteen years in Tanishq Retail Operations before heading Retail for

Taneira, Titan's ethnic-wear business. He remembers grooming standards being a big part of the Tanishq service flow: how to wear a saree, how to tie a tie, what lipstick to wear, etc. and getting a big pushback from the staff and franchisees from cities like Patna. *We are already perceived as a high-end brand. If we start wearing ties and makeup, we will be perceived to be elitist. Bihar ka jeweller nahi maanenge! (They won't think of us as local!)* Anirban and all other field managers had to keep at it for months, for store teams to appreciate the importance of these things. They also used Titan's ex-services colleagues to train the store security guards in the niceties of smiling at customers and wishing them as they opened and closed the doors. Some of our company store staff who we could influence better as well as some of the customer-oriented franchisee partners became the catalysts for this change of mindset.

'We had some hilarious but challenging consequences,' chortles Munish Chawla, another Retail Operations veteran who now heads the Mega Stores programme for Tanishq. The information that we collected from customers was quite comprehensive and personal. One item of information was about the music that the customer liked, which we would use later to send a CD on the customer's birthday. Munish remembers one situation where two customers who were friends had met somewhere. One of them came to know that the other had received a Kishore Kumar music CD from Tanishq, which had been sent on his birthday. This first customer, who thought he was buying more jewellery from us than the second, was quite upset that he had not been sent a Kishore Kumar CD as well. Munish cracks up while he shares with me how they had to struggle to convince him that he was being sent a Mohammed Rafi CD on his birthday which was down the road, as Rafi was the singer he had indicated on the form! But he was not convinced; he wanted his Kishore Kumar CD! Munish is quite tickled by these memories. 'One customer stormed into our Delhi's South Extension store one day and complained that we had forgotten to send a cake home for her birthday!'

Our staff resisted the whole process of collecting such information. To start with, they were not convinced about the utility of the effort and, on top of that, it gave them additional work as they had to fill out the forms themselves. We had to persist with it for quite some time till the repeat purchases from those customers started building the belief. And, over time, other stores became convinced looking at the better sales performance of these stores which had better customer metrics behind them.

How much do we know about our customers as individuals? Do we know what festivals they celebrate?

Do we know if their twenty-fifth anniversary falls in 2024? Do we know if it is Kishore Kumar's music they love to listen to or Mohammed Rafi's? Do we know anything about their children? In today's digital world, these things have become much easier to capture. In fact, companies can build this information over time, using the apps to their advantage.

Between 2007 and 2012, the seeds for this intense and continuous customer focus had been sown. But as we were becoming much larger, with a larger number of franchisee partners and store staff, we needed to build deep processes to capture customer information as well as deliver customer delight at scale.

We had learnt over the years that the traditional jewellers had built very good relationships with their customers. That approach started with the owner of the store who personally knew many of the high-value customers and trickled down to many of the store staff as well. However, the initial approach in Tanishq had been different, where the staff had been taught to be more 'professional', approaching the customers only when the customers sought their help, otherwise leaving them to themselves. The original 'art gallery' perception was also for encouraging customers to browse without any help. But as we began to move into the centre of the jewellery market, into the wedding jewellery space, our store experience needed to dramatically change. The staff had to move to a 'lean forward' approach of dealing with the customers, proactively understanding customer requirements, treating all types of customers alike, having significant patience with each of them, not exactly pushing them to close the purchase fast, having the right knowledge about products, policies, processes, etc. Around 2012, we decided that all this had to be done with great efficiency and at scale. For the creation of fans to happen, we needed staff with the right profile. We needed a systematic process of engagement with every customer at every touchpoint, we needed to train all staff members and all our franchisee partners in it. We needed to measure the actual customer satisfaction in every store. We also needed to conduct mystery audits to identify execution gaps.

This programme was called the Tanishq Way of Life.

The mystery audit was a critical part of the Tanishq Way of Life. Trained assessors, working for a partner company, would visit every Tanishq store once a month, posing as a customer. They would go through the entire process of exploration, shortlisting and buying jewellery. They would assess how the store staff engaged with them, from greeting them at the door to understanding their requirements to explaining the products, policies, processes and so on. The actual performance of the staff would be compared with the SOP that was laid down and the store would be rated accordingly and informed about it every month.

The store staff found smart ways to counter any low mystery audit scores: *the staff member was new; the auditor came on a rush day so we could not pay enough attention and so on.* 'I remember some stores requesting me to inform them about the day of the mystery audit so that they can be better prepared for it,' chuckles Anirban. 'We really had to stay with it for months and months to embed them into our operations.'

The emphasis on retail operational excellence should be entirely attributed to Sandeep Kulhalli. Sandeep moved into Tanishq in 2008 to head Retail and Marketing and helped establish many foundational aspects of operations. Reputed as a very demanding but fair leader, totally outcome and business-focused, unsentimental and unafraid to stand alone in his convictions, Sandeep's lasting impact is visible even today.

I remember a monthly review in 2016 or so, we were discussing non-conversions. This was the part of the store traffic that walked out without buying anything. It was close to 25 per cent of the people who came into our stores. Sandeep made this telling point that so much recovery opportunity was sitting within this 25 per cent (after all, they had come so close to buying). He pushed the regional managers, area managers and store managers to build a comprehensive process to understand the reasons for non-purchase. In many cases, it was to do with the customers not finding the right product. Capturing this reason in a concrete way (*not enough choice in the handmade bangle category, in the 10-to-15-gram weight range, for example*) helped the stores to try and intervene quickly. Sandeep's satisfaction is quite evident. 'The stores would look for such stock in nearby stores or even in warehouses, then call the customers with that information, request them to come back after a couple of days and end up completing that sale. During some months, this 'recovery' would be as high as 3 per cent of the total sale!'

This approach was not just beneficial to the company. The customers were also impressed with the efforts taken by the company to reach out to them and invite them back.

For thousands of staff to behave spontaneously in that manner, we had to light a fire in their hearts. My talk to the store staff in the huddle was to light this fire, a glowing light about this glorious purpose. 'Over time, when the customer continues to walk out of the store with a smile all around, she ceases to be a customer. You are no longer a salesperson. You become their *saheli* (friend), their *beti* (daughter) or *bhanja* (nephew). The relationship becomes very personal, very special,' I continue, building the rationale. 'Then the customers start entering their relatives' house, not a jewellery store. They end up spending a couple of hours with their *behen* (sister) and end up buying some jewellery while they are at it! Wouldn't this be a wonderful thing to create? Wouldn't it also give you great joy at work?' This rationale has intrinsic merit, and the staff started nodding. Some of them echoed my sentiment and started sharing their own customer delight stories.

It was sometime in 2013 or so. I was in a customer meet at our Khar, Mumbai, store. It's our smallest store in Mumbai, just about 1,200 square feet. It is quite cramped, considering it's spread over two floors. There are about ten customers in the meet, all women. During the conversation, I come to know that one of the customers lived very close to our Andheri store, also in Mumbai, which is the largest store in the country – of about 22,000 square feet. We opened the Andheri store in 2011, two years back. I asked that lady if she was aware of the Andheri store. She said she was. To this I expressed my surprise. The Andheri store housed more varieties of jewellery than the Khar store. It even had a large canteen, a children's play area, multiple sofas to relax for as long as you wanted and many parking slots. Moreover, it was less than a kilometre from her house! Yet she shopped at Khar, some 7 kilometres farther!

She smiled, 'Yes, the Andheri store has everything. Except Himanshu. You transfer Himanshu from this store to Andheri, I will start going there the next day!' Himanshu was a salesperson in our Khar store. He was present in the room with us and started smiling as the customer was sharing this. That's when the power of this potential hit me. The loyalty is not just to the brand, not just to a specific store of the brand, but also to a specific salesperson of the store! This incident reinforces the '*saheli*', '*beti*', '*bhanja*' sentiment in my mind and the Himanshu story travels with me to all the corners of India over the next ten years, to inspire thousands of sales staff.

'Mrs Bhatia has been our customer for more than fifteen years. We are so close, I feel like a part of her family,' the words tumble out of Gopi Panchal. Gopi is a star salesperson (senior retail sales officer) in one of our Ahmedabad stores. Mrs Bhatia wanted a diamond necklace for her son's wedding. It was 2006 or 2007. The store did not have much variety in those days, especially in the price bands she was looking for. She was not satisfied with the collection available in that store or even the other Tanishq stores in Ahmedabad. Nor was she okay with ordering from a catalogue. She wanted to see the piece. Gopi was stuck. Then she suddenly remembered a necklace that she had sold to another customer, a doctor, a few months back. Gopi felt that Mrs Bhatia would like that piece. She reached out to that doctor, gave her the background and asked her if she could borrow that piece. The doctor suggested that Gopi bring Mrs Bhatia to her home instead. Gopi took Mrs Bhatia to the doctor's house. Mrs Bhatia fell in love with that piece and immediately placed an order for it. She was delighted with Gopi's initiative and has remained a loyal customer of the store all these years, despite living 300 kilometres away. Gopi is pleased as punch, 'She has asked me so many times to visit her home, which I haven't been able to. Sometime back she brought me a silver chalice from Vrindavan, with a Krishna Lalla idol on it, thanking me for "*sukh-dukh mein saath rehene ke liye*" (for being with us through thick and thin).' Gopi is surely part of Mrs Bhatia's family!

How proactive and helpful are the people who deal with your customers? How much are they bound by the circumstances, rules or processes that are laid out? And how much motivation, passion and energy do they have to break out of all those to serve their customers?

It was the second wave of Covid, sometime in June 2021. The MI Road, Jaipur, Tanishq store had a customer whose daughter was soon going to get married. The daughter wanted the mother to be central to the jewellery selection, but they did not want to bring her to the store since she wasn't well and they did not want to bother other customers. The staff could have done video calls, but that was not good enough for the family. Pawan Sharma, a salesperson (retail sales officer) in that Tanishq store, decided to open the store exclusively for the family. Three of the sales staff and the security guard went to the store early morning, had it sanitized thoroughly and were ready for the family sharp at 8:30 a.m. (the store opened to the public at 10 a.m.). The lady, accompanied by her husband and two daughters, spent an hour in the showroom. Pawan had this organized a second time and the family were able to select the wedding jewellery to their satisfaction. 'They were so delighted with this option! We were invited to the wedding, of course, but we could not go. I sent a bouquet,' Pawan's quiet pride is visible.

Vishal Saraogi, business manager for all the jewellery stores of Manoj Parasrampuria, our partner in Kolkata, has this unusual story about a Bengali lady customer who came one day to our Kankurgachi store looking a little troubled. It was sometime in 2022. She had been their customer for fifteen years. Vishal asked her what the issue was. She told him that her daughter just got engaged. Vishal congratulated her and enquired why she looked worried. She told him that her husband was a quiet, gentle person and she was worried about the wedding arrangements, and whether they would both be able to cope, especially since the groom was from another state and another culture. 'Without thinking, I told her, "Madam, it's also my sister's wedding, na? Leave it to me!"' Vishal tells me. Over the next few weeks, Vishal and Sanjeev (a colleague from the store) helped organize the wedding hall, the caterer, the stay for the groom and his family and even the return gifts and took the load off the family. Manoj our franchisee partner, helped with his car and suggestions. The wedding went very well. 'The customer's husband made us stand in the centre of the hall, with the guests all around us and started talking about the things we did for the wedding and people kept clapping. The groom and his family also had many things to say about us. We were so touched and embarrassed!' recollects Vishal.

'I remember a customer meet in 2021 or 2022,' recalls CEO Ajoy Chawla. 'One customer said, *"Aap ka problem sirf do hai. Ek rate ka. Aur ek weight ka!"* (*You have just two problems. Your jewellery's prices and their weight!*) I think this was a male customer. I smiled at them and started justifying the price of Tanishq and everything we do for the *karigar*s. Then a lady customer, she must have been seventy or so, told me that *all that* is your responsibility as a Tata Company, so don't pass on that cost to us! It was almost like a wise parent chiding an errant son!'

This kind of relationship with customers is a unique aspect of Tanishq. Over the years, hundreds of thousands of customers have become like family members to our staff and our franchisee partners as well. They don't feel like buying the jewellery if their favourite salesperson is absent on the day of their visit and sometimes wait for them to come back from their leave. They drop into the store quite often, just to have coffee and spend time with them. When a salesperson is a little behind on her target, she calls her favourite customer for help, by buying into the latest collection!

And all this has been done at scale. The Net Promoter Score (NPS, the globally recognized Customer Advocacy measure) stands at a very impressive eighty-five, a global benchmark number. This means that thousands of sales and service staff in the stores are delivering customer delight time after time, day after day, enabled by the multiple training processes and driven by the fire in their hearts to continuously create smiles and advocates.

The Anuttara programme of Tanishq morphed into the Encircle loyalty programme at the Titan Company level around 2013 (covering all businesses of Titan Company) and has developed into a powerhouse loyalty programme that combines data, analytics and relationships to deliver sales, minimize dormancy and build customer advocacy.

'When a customer writes to us with a problem, it really bothers us, disturbs us,' sums up Ajoy. 'Even though the company machinery will swing into action to address the issue, I feel like writing to the customer myself or talking to her and making it right. Only when that happens do I get closure.'

3

Partnership

How naturally does stakeholder capitalism come to the leaders in the organization? Are vendors and franchisees true partners in a fulfilling, magical common journey or are they mere tools that are tolerated till they are useful?

One could say that Titan Company is India's most experienced franchising company. The founders realized that to achieve the revolution that they had dreamed up for the watch category, the country had to be dotted with dozens of exclusive showrooms (called the Titan World today), delivering a consistent customer experience encompassing a stunning, wide product range, impressive visual presentation, consistent company policies and programmes and a very warm, memorable store experience. It had become clear by the late 1980s, soon after the first

Titan franchisee showroom opened in Vijayawada, that this scale could be achieved with speed *only through franchisees*. Titan was also clear that it made strategic sense, while also being philosophically correct, to treat the franchisees as partners and not as 'dealers'.

What do we mean when we say that treating the franchisee as a partner makes strategic sense? With *any partner*, it's always two-way. It works the same way in a company-partner situation. We don't take the partner for granted. For any important decision we take, we involve the partner in the discussion. The partner has the right to give inputs and feedback to the company to make everything better. All this makes for a virtuous improvement cycle, which is very much needed especially when the franchisee is the bridge between the company and its customers and understands the local competition much better. On the philosophical front, it's all about a human approach towards everyone who works with you, a desire to share the prosperity that the company generates with others who are part of it and a focus on delivering that prosperity constantly. This strategic and philosophical approach to partnering has made Titan Company India's most successful franchising company, with more than 1,000 franchisees as of 2023, running more than 2,300 stores and contributing to more than two-thirds of Titan's revenue.

The Tanishq Story

The franchisees of Tanishq have been at the forefront of the growth of the brand almost from day one. Over the twenty-five years since the first franchisee was signed up, close to 270 franchisee partners have helped set up more than 400 stores across the length and breadth of India and taken Tanishq into the smallest of towns possible. In all these places, they have been the eyes and ears of the company, providing critical inputs for us to serve our customers much better. They have been the stamp of reassurance to the many customers to whom Tanishq was unknown, especially in those early days. They were Tanishq's bridge to HNI, or high net-worth individual, families whom they knew or could reach and, most importantly, they have been the brand ambassadors of Tanishq wherever the stores are.

What are the pros and cons of franchising at scale?

Pros:
- A company can use the huge pool of entrepreneurs across India and plant its flags at a faster clip.
- It can build an asset and opex (operational expenditure) light model that comes in very handy in managing business cycles better.
- It builds a stronger voice in the market. A franchisee from a small town would have a greater influence on

company policy and strategy than the manager of a company store from the same town, who would be a junior in the hierarchy.

Cons:
- Standard delivery of customer experience could be a challenge.
- Over a long time, as the scale builds in every store, the company may end up leaving some money on the table, which it could have kept if every store was its own.

In Titan's view, the pros have always outweighed the cons. Other than in large metro cities, we have depended on franchisee partners for scaling the business and have built deep processes for standardizing customer experience.

I had said earlier, that one of the dimensions of strategic partnering was to get inputs and feedback from partners. Active listening was key to that. In 2010, we set up franchisee panels to enable this. This was an annual event, with two sets of ten to twelve franchisees spending half a day each with the leaders and heads of departments of Tanishq, in Bengaluru. In this four-hour meeting, the franchisees would raise multiple issues and offer many suggestions and improvements, all to increase sales, strengthen the brand value, improve customer experience, make store operations less cumbersome and deliver more financial value to their businesses as well. Having been in every one of these panel meetings since the beginning, I can say with total conviction how crucial this programme was for the continued success of Tanishq.

'I will sit on this side,' says Bhaskar. We are all in the conference room of Titan Company, the franchisees sitting on one side of the table and all of us on the other side, in the first meeting of this programme. The twinkle in his trademark smile underscores Bhaskar's gentle hint to the Jewellery division management (me as CEO along with the other leaders of Tanishq) about which side the MD of the company is on. By sitting on the franchisee side of the table and with those words, Bhaskar has reminded all of us how we run things in Titan.

This partnership approach has continued for more than two decades now. Through the formal processes of the franchisee panels and regional cascades (four of them for the four regions), as well as through direct conversations of various HQ and region management levels with the partners, continuous visits to all the stores, the voice of the partner and the voice of the market have been heard loud and clear. Strategies, tactics, policies and processes have been debated before implementation or modified after experimentation through an approach of total ownership, through total involvement.

Corrections in gold rates and making charges, changes in gold exchange policies, introduction of jewellery at low making charge levels, introduction of open *polki* collections, making large *jhumkas* (a type of earring) for Punjab and parts of North India, expansion of the product range in high-value diamond jewellery, bringing in traditional products like '*vedhni*' for Maharashtra, celebrating '*chhath pooja*' in Bihar, giving 'karva chauth' national importance, adding details in invoices for complete transparency, designing/modifying store staff incentives – the number of improvements that were done using the feedback from the partners goes on and on.

Manoj Parsrampuria is one of Tanishq's long-standing franchisees in Kolkata. Manoj acknowledges that he never felt that he was an associate or partner of the company; he always felt that he was an owner of the brand and the company, more like a family member running a branch. Everything in his store was the same as everywhere else, all the policies and processes were identical and they were never made to feel different. Manoj smiles, 'And it went beyond work also. When I called Bhaskar in 2017 to tell him about my daughter's marriage, he said, "You mean my niece's?"'

Jogu Prasad is Titan Company's first-ever franchisee partner, opening the first Titan Watches franchisee showroom in Vijayawada in 1988 (her Tanishq store in Vijayawada opened in 1998). These thirty-five years have created a deep relationship between the company and Jogu and her family. On a recent visit to Vijayawada, I ended up clicking a very special picture with her, her daughter Smita and granddaughter Shivi. I have known Smita since 1993. Joining us in the picture were Mrs Bramaramba, a loyal customer for decades, Srivani, her daughter and a customer herself and Diya, her granddaughter and seven-year-old vlogger who posted her first reel on Tanishq a few days before this photo was shot. Three generations from the franchisee side and three from the customer side!

Many people spend many, many years working in Titan (it's my thirty-fourth year as I write this) and, on account of that, most people end up spending considerable time with our partners. We even end up going to many of their homes, have a meal with them, get to know their families as well. A beautiful relationship, quite outside the dimensions of work, builds through all these interactions, leading to a 'family' feeling all around, that's very difficult to describe. This feeling influences how the company and the partners look at each other, behave with each other, leading to commitment, loyalty and advocacy of a very high order.

Jatin Parekh, our Ahmedabad franchisee partner and one of the spokespersons for the franchisee community, recalls that his first Tanishq store opened in 1997 and Bhaskar inaugurated it. He also remembers David Saldanha flying down to the store a few weeks later, for the Lakshmi Puja. It was almost as if a family member who was out of town had flown down specially for this puja. Jatin smiles, 'It hasn't changed in twenty-five years! Whether Govind Raj and team flying down for my daughter Amisha's wedding in 2005 or my granddaughter Aastha being in touch with you, Venkat, for her project in 2021 – it's always been like a family feeling!'

The franchisee partners often speak of their staff as family and the staff also return the favour. The customers often speak of the staff as family and speak of the franchisees in the same vein. The company employees and franchisee partners often refer to each other in these 'family' terms. Is it all some sentimental mishmash?

Rainy and Harinder Madaan come from Amritsar. Their Tanishq store opened in 2001. Harinder talks about how the relationship between their staff and their customers is also like one large family. One day, their store manager Jatin was in the Amritsar court for some bail-evidence related work that he had been called for. He was prepared to spend the whole day in the court for this.

Just after half an hour, he heard the judge calling out to him, '*Arre Jatin, yahaan kaise aana hua?* How come you are here, Jatin?. The judge was a Tanishq customer and Jatin was rather pleased to be recognized by him in the court.

Sometime in 2021, I was on my first visit to Ambikapur, a small town in Chhattisgarh. After the inauguration of the Tanishq store, we were invited to the home of Abhishek Garg, the young franchisee, for lunch. The family turned out to be Marwari, whose cuisine I cannot have enough of! The feast was sumptuous and delicious and included *hari mirch ka achhaar* (green chilli pickle) and *adrak ke tukde* (slivers of fresh ginger). I was amazed at the entire meal, especially about these two condiments. Seeing this, Suruchi, the thoughtful wife of Abhishek, packed a bottle each of the pickle and the ginger for me to take back. When the MD of a company is given a gift (maybe an expensive pen?), there is a certain relationship that the gift evokes. When the MD is given a bottle of pickle to take away, what does she or he become to the people who are giving it?

Let's now move to our partners on the production side.

It was in the early days of my move into Tanishq. I was in Kolkata, sometime in late 2005 or early 2006. So far, my impression of Tanishq had been one of elegance (the jewellery), grandeur (the stores), innovation (the plant), camaraderie (the office) and professionalism (meetings with vendor partners in our own offices). I didn't realize that I was about to get jolted out of my life in the next ten minutes. We were in Sinthi More, one of the biggest jewellery-making hubs of Kolkata. LRN, some other colleagues and myself had gone to visit the workshops where our vendors made our gold jewellery. It was summer and the temperature was in the high forties. It was quite a crowded place with narrow streets and narrower alleys, looking like a scene from the early twentieth century. Perhaps very little has changed since then. We entered a multistorey building. We were told that some of the rooms in this building were rented out to our head *karigar*s, rooms in which the bench *karigar*s (those who make the jewellery) worked. Our vendors acted as the aggregators of such head *karigar*s and were the bridge between the company and the centres of production, being responsible for product quality, delivery and gold safety. We climbed to the second floor. The staircase was narrow, and the walls were stained with paan spit. We reached the landing and entered a small room (10 feet x 10 feet, at best). Even as I was entering the room, I saw a tin sheet door of a toilet on the side and felt the faint whiff of urine. Some of my local colleagues and the vendors were a bit embarrassed and were trying to form a cordon around the 'dignitaries' from Bengaluru.

It's been nearly twenty years since that visit, but I just need to close my eyes today to evoke that scene – the plaster had peeled off from the walls, there was one window which overlooked a kind of courtyard of the building and the ceiling was not beyond 9 feet high. Four small tube lights hung from the ceiling at 5 feet height and provided the light for the workshop. You had to bend a little if you didn't want to bump into the tube lights. There were two nylon ropes strung across the room at the same height on which hung *lungi*s and shirts. Eight *karigar*s were sitting on the floor making jewellery; there were tools and components strewn on the floor. Some of them were assembling the jewellery, some were using torches to solder parts, a few in their *lungi*s, many in their underpants, almost all bare-chested to beat the heat. The ironic thing was the smile with which they all greeted us. A smile so effulgent that it dwarfed the tube lights. Their '*nomoshkar*' dissolved the gloom in that place. They showed us the Tanishq jewellery they were making. The beauty of each piece transported us to another place. I asked them where they have their lunch. They pointed to the dabbas in the corner and told me that, come lunchtime, they simply clear the things on the floor, have lunch and reorganize the place back for work. I nodded, thinking, *what was I expecting?*

We looked at a few more places like this. They were no different – carbon copies of the first – including the joy of the *karigar*s and the beauty of the Tanishq necklaces. As we left Sinthi More for our lunch and went back to the office, we were all understandably quiet. I kept thinking, 'How can such exquisite jewellery come out of such wretched circumstances? How can we sell a necklace for Rs 5 lakh to a lady from our elegant Camac Street showroom and still have this situation continue?' These were the questions running in my mind. I was jolted, bothered and burning to do something about this. LRN's heart and mind were equally aligned to this issue. He came up with a powerful phrase: *Bring a smile to the karigar's face.*

Over the years, various programmes have been created in this direction. Unnatti, Mr Perfect, Mr Perfect+, 4–P. Significant milestones are reached.

Remember, this awareness came to us in 2006, when Tanishq was less than 2 per cent of its current scale. It was more about our burning desire to make a difference in the *karigar*s' lives than our ability at that time to make it. It was our conscience that was impelling us, not our bank balance. It was about stakeholder capitalism.

Before and after in the same vendor partner unit: The transformation in the life of the karigar *(artisan) is one of the lasting legacies of Tanishq.*

Is an apparel company thinking about the men and women who are working for its vendor partners, making the clothes it sells? Is it bothered by the conditions in which they work? Are its leaders visiting those centres of manufacturing?

How can a food delivery and ride-hail company, even a start-up, think about its delivery people and drivers? Do they sleep adequately, do they eat on time or eat hot food?

Everything begins with that empathy.

In 2012, we opened the Karigar Centre in Hosur. It was a landmark project in our transformation journey. To start with, it was a fabulous-looking imposing structure, with room for four self-contained karigar parks (fifty to seventy-five *karigars* could work in each karigar park). Very well-designed bays, where *karigars* could sit and work in comfort, with the right kind of temperature control and the best of tools and processes for efficiency. The gas cylinders were kept outside the building for safety. Many of the *karigars* were from Bengal. I told our Karigar Centre team that we should get a Bengali cook for the canteen so that the *karigars* can get their *luchi* aloo and *jhal muri* (typical Bengali breakfast and snacks) a few times every week. I also asked them to organize a daily delivery of *Anandabazar Patrika*. Why not some carrom boards and chess boards too? Much of this happened at the inauguration and our most special guest was the president of the Kolkata Karigar Union.

Now, to go back to my early stint in Tanishq – the middle of 2005.

Akila from the Merchandizing department came to me with the news that we had signed up with the Shah Rukh Khan–Rani Mukerji film, *Paheli*, and we needed to make *kundan* jewellery for the movie. *I ask her 'What is kundan jewellery?'* Her expression was priceless. Then we reached out to the factory sourcing team. They also asked us what is this *kundan* jewellery! In the next couple of months, we somehow scrambled and got pieces made for the movie. *Paheli* was a reasonable success and Tanishq got known for serious jewellery.

Slowly, I started understanding the supply chain of Tanishq. Nearly 90 per cent of our gold jewellery and 70 per cent of our diamond jewellery were made by our vendors. In the watch industry, Titan was the last word in innovation and quality because watchmaking was a technology-intensive process. Titan had the best people to design the processes and had the money to invest in the best machines, particularly for the watch movements and cases and assembly. But, unlike watches, most Indian jewellery was made by people with skill, assisted by low-tech machines. This meant that innovation and quality

Stakeholder focus comes alive vividly in the details of the approach. Bengali food and Bengali news delight the karigars *in their home away from home in Hosur, Tamil Nadu.*

were not the preserve of a big company like Titan, but were spread across a large vendor ecosystem including some small, very specialized small firms. This meant that we needed to develop an integrated production system that recognized and respected the various roles many vendors had to play.

Colin Shah is the founder and MD of Kama Jewellery, ex-chairman of the Gem & Jewellery Export Promotion Council and a vendor partner of Tanishq. He highlights that no jewellery company is as interested in building systems and processes in a vendor's place as Titan. He vividly recollects that when the World's Best Quality programme (to upgrade the quality of Tanishq jewellery and take it to world-class levels) was implemented in his factory a few years back, he asked Anikesh Nandy (then head of Quality at Tanishq) why Tanishq was doing this with vendors who also worked for many other Indian retailers. Nandy had replied, *'We don't think like that. For us, strategic partnering is very real. The overall benefits of the programme are worth the risk of our sharing openly.'*

Sanjay Dugar heads the Vijay Trading Corporation (VTC), one of our strategic partners in Kolkata. Sanjay acknowledges that Titan has done as much for the *karigar*s as it has done for the vendor partners. Through all these years, their manufacturing has been transformed as much as the lives of the *karigar*s. Provident Fun (PF), Employees' State Insurance (ESI), hygienic working conditions, quality of food and drinking water, indoor air quality, acid disposal – all these really touched the *karigar*s emotionally and spiritually. The majority of the *karigar*s with every vendor started shifting their allegiance to Tanishq. Sanjay shares, '70 per cent of my *karigar*s have been dedicated to Tanishq for so many years now. They feel proud about Tanishq and are willing to take up any improvement that the Tanishq team brings in.'

Some memories are burnt in our souls. It was sometime in 2016 or 2017. We were all in Imagica, a theme park outside Mumbai, celebrating our Karigar Connect programme. Some 50 of us from Tanishq, all our Mumbai vendor partners and some 800 of their *karigar*s. It was a full-day event of fun for the *karigar*s in the theme park, ending with awards and entertainment in the evening. Many of us were standing on a high platform at the third-floor level, lighting a lamp to kickstart the day. The ground level was full of snow, created by a huge snow machine. Hundreds of *karigar*s were running on it, making snowballs and throwing at each other, taking selfies. The atmosphere was delirious, childlike and infectious. It was also a visual spectacle, enhanced by the hundreds of red, blue, orange and yellow t-shirts that the *karigar*s wore. This Karigar Connect idea was born from a similar programme that we had started for our retail store staff in 2008, called Face-to-Face, an evening for recognition, celebration and partying, which has since then become a solid annual feature.

Kapil Soni is a tall and handsome vendor partner from Jaipur who now runs Finesse, an expert *kundan* jewellery firm. The firm Kapil worked for made some of the jewellery Tanishq created for *Jodhaa Akbar* in 2007. He recollects that there was a beautiful necklace with a swan pendant (which later became quite visible in the publicity material featuring Aishwarya Rai), which was being made by another vendor. They were not able to do it well and the Tanishq team had got into a jam. Anjali Sikka, the designer, had asked Kapil for help. The time was hopelessly short, just four days! 'But how could I say no? Titan was family, after all!' Kapil smiles, showing off his 'T' tattoo on his arm. 'We worked night and day and created an exquisite piece just in time. My reward was taking the piece with Anjali to the hotel and meeting Ashutosh Gowariker and Aishwarya Rai!'

We are perhaps the only retailer in the world who entertains *its vendors*. It's almost always the reverse with all others. It's unusual for a company to invite all competing vendors together time after time, letting them mingle freely, letting them share strategies, practices and policies. We do this for our vendor 'BAM', the most recent one being in Barcelona in 2022. I have observed that *competitors* have become close friends over the years, seeking mutual help from each other. The BAMs have greatly helped the vendor partners understand the strategy of Tanishq and how all of them need to align with those. Great bonding with the Tanishq teams happens at those events and open houses with the senior leadership of Tanishq help us improve our ways of working together better. All these remind me of the slew of things that Tanishq has done with the vendors, with the total involvement of each one of them: the streamlining of the input drawings like the Product Information Sheet (PIS) and the Product Development Information Sheet (PDIS), the standardization of the gauge thickness of the gold wires, the preparation of the Bill of Materials, the component centre to supply a full kit, the use of the well-known Theory of Constraints for smooth flow of material, programmes like the three-day miracle to substantially reduce lead time, the focus on product innovation and Vendor Product Innovation Meets, the introduction of Lean, 5S, Six Sigma principles to increase efficiency and improve effectiveness, the 4-P programme in the late 2010s, the continuous focus on the *karigar*s' capability building, comfort and convenience, dignity and future, income and welfare – it has been an unbelievable partnership!

P. Radhamanalan retired as the vice president of Gold Jewellery Manufacturing and Responsible Sourcing in September 2023, after thirty-four years in Titan. Radha, as he was fondly called, was the driving force behind the array of transformation programmes that Tanishq had created in partnership with vendors over the years. First, it was the Unnatti programme around 2006, then it was Mr Perfect starting in 2008. The Karigar Centre was opened in 2012. The 4-P programme was conceived around 2018 when Radha's department changed its name to Responsible Sourcing Department. 'The 4-P programme was the crowning glory of our manufacturing transformation,' says Radha.

The concepts of the 4-P programme are quite impressive. To start with, the 4-Ps themselves: People, Place, Process, Planet. A total of 124 initiatives/steps define the 'Tanishq Way' of jewellery making, ranging from PF/ESI practices (People) to acid disposal (Planet) that each vendor should follow. Then each vendor is rated on those 124 steps to get a synthesized rating that ranges from cottage to basic to standard to world-class. The 4-P programme was envisioned to move all our vendor partners to the standard level in five years.

C.K. Venkataraman

More than 90 per cent of the *karigar*s today work inside a 4-P set-up: decent and predictable incomes, a comfortable environment with good ergonomics, convenient and effective processes, safe working conditions and good retirement benefits. The dream that began in Sinthi More nearly two decades back could travel this far only because Titan Company views its vendors as its valuable partners and sees the *karigar*s in the same way as it sees its employees.

Over the decades, the 'integrated' supply chain of Tanishq has remained integrated, with considerable jewellery innovation and output continuing to come from vendor partners, reinforcing the 'equal' role played by them nearly thirty years after the brand was launched. While this underscores the role naturally played by the vendors in a skill category like jewellery, it is also a testament to how Titan views its stakeholders in general.

So, the question is: how do you view your vendors? As suppliers who are at your beck and call? An unequal part of the value chain who are there to be used till they are useful and discarded when not perceived to be so? Or strategic partners in whose development the company constantly invests, enabling them to continue to play a critical role in the company's success?

4

People

How does the organization think and feel about its employees? Are they just factors of production or sales? Or are they members of a large family that looks out for each other, caring and sharing for each other, without compromising the highest standards of performance that they have set out for themselves?

Bhaskar Bhat, MD of Titan for seventeen years, found the term human resources inappropriate. 'Resources are those things that you maximize and, when they are no longer useful to you, you junk them. *People* have hearts, they have feelings and we can't treat people like resources! So, HR is the wrong term for that department!' Titan did treat its employees as people, right from its inception. But the term HR lingered on for many years till an opportune moment came to change that.

Was Bhaskar just being clever in his turn of phrase? Was he mixing up the priorities of a business enterprise? Wasn't he letting sentimentality complicate rationale?

If we go back to the history of the Tata Group, you can see this thread running through the groups' actions. Some of the Tata companies had PF, ESI and even a creche for young mothers in the early twentieth century, way before anyone else had them. Employees had been placed by the Tata Group at the centre of their stakeholder focus, along with partners, society, government and the environment. Without saying it as much, the Tatas had always considered employees as *people*.

So did Titan. Way back in 1986, Titan managers had gone into the villages around Hosur, Tamil Nadu, and recruited young girls and boys who had completed their tenth standard. They came from challenging circumstances. None of their family members had worked in a company like Titan, certainly no women. Titan trained these enthusiastic employees in watchmaking and built a world-class manufacturing plant in Hosur. Most of those employees are in their early fifties today, continuing to work in Titan in Hosur. Titan made a similar effort in 1994 for its jewellery plant in Hosur as well.

The second jewellery factory of Titan, and the first in northern India, was set up in Dehradun in 2005. The third one followed in Pantnagar, also in Uttarakhand, in 2012. Continuing its philosophy and practice, Titan had gone into the villages around the Pantnagar area to recruit and train young women in jewellery making. About 140 young women were recruited and trained for this prestigious plant, overcoming the anxiety of the parents about the safety and future of their daughters. However, like every other unit of Titan, the future of these young people became assured and comfortable.

Anikesh Nandy is the AVP of Diamond Jewellery Manufacturing and Sourcing at Titan's Jewellery division and was the head of the Pantnagar unit for many years. 'Every day, a couple of young women would faint. The van was always on standby to take them to the hospital,' Nandy recalls. This was around 2014. Nandy and the team wondered what the issue was. They consulted the doctors. The common root cause was low haemoglobin. They were a bit surprised since most of these women were from the hills and were used to being active. Why was their haemoglobin low? Nandy and his team came to know that most of them were skipping breakfast when coming to work. They decided that they needed to step in and help. They started giving everyone breakfast and then supplemented the lunch menu with greens and chickpeas. After a few weeks, they started measuring the haemoglobin levels. The women became much stronger, the fainting stopped and then became a distant memory. Nandy's relief and satisfaction are palpable. 'Many other manufacturing units in Pantnagar followed our practice and hundreds of employees benefited.'

Do we care enough about our employees? They are neither resources nor investments and certainly not costs. They are People. But thinking of your team or employees as people does not just mean ensuring they are well looked after. How do we professionally treat the people around us?

In a typical discussion about the future leaders of the company, one of my senior colleagues would say about a candidate, 'He needs to develop a higher level of drive.' Bhaskar would gently comment, 'He's so innovative!' I would say about another person, 'He is a bit idealistic.' Again, Bhaskar would take the discussion somewhere else, 'I have not seen interpersonal skills like what he has anywhere else in Titan.' Ever so politely, but rather firmly, he would steer the conversation around what each person was exceptionally good at. 'Why don't we focus entirely on what someone is very good at and not worry, perhaps even ignore, what she or he cannot do well enough?' was what he was telling us.

Each of us is good at *something*. Some of us can

synthesize many things into a single concept and create believers. Some of us can drum up energy and make the rest of us march towards a goal with purpose. Some of us can run a tight ship, delivering exceptional efficiency, time after time. Some of us always have new ideas and can get others to come up with them as well. *That core* defines our leaning, our natural style. And that defines our persona, creates our success and builds our reputation. But that leaning and that style also means that we are 'weak' in some other area, which offers the potential to make each one of us well-rounded. In pursuit of that well-roundedness, many of us give feedback to those who are in our teams, to 'fix' those gaps and become much more effective. While in principle there is nothing wrong with that goal, some of us can become fixated with that goal so much that we lose overall perspective. These leanings and styles are often deep-rooted, especially in managers who are over forty. Constant pressure on them to correct a couple of the gaps ends up with them second-guessing themselves all the time and faltering in those aspects where they are exceptionally good.

Bhaskar's counterpoints made me question my approach to this subject. I started ignoring 'gaps' in my colleagues' priorities or styles unless they were deal-breakers (they rarely are). This new approach liberated them and they ended up maximizing what they were naturally so good at, thereby, maximizing the benefits for the organization.

Focus only on what each person is good at; try to ignore what you think that person needs to do better.

How can you do multiple things in your organization that make your employees emotionally attached to the organization?

Rajnarayan was chief human resources officer (CHRO) of Titan Company from 2011 till 2021. 'Around 2014 or so, I am not sure when exactly, we had decided to close our Dehradun jewellery plant,' recollects Raj. That plant had been in operation for ten years, but, with a much bigger plant having come up in Pantnagar in the same state and the inability to turn the Dehradun plant into an integrated plant on account of greenbelt constraints, the reasons for continuing the plant had dwindled. As part of the closure, we offered a Voluntary Retirement Scheme (VRS) for the forty-odd employees. For those who chose not to take the VRS, we were to work on getting them roles in the Pantnagar unit or other offices of the Jewellery division. The production employees were quite young, in their late twenties, and they saw the decision as unfair to them and were insisting that the company continue its operations in Dehradun. We did not want to do that. Matters were coming to a head when Raj went to Dehradun to meet all of them. He invited them to a conference room and told them that the decision was final, but he was willing to listen to them, understand the issues and solve them.

He asked each of them to put down their requirement on a piece of paper and put it in a box. He told them that he would pick out each one, read it out aloud and then tell them if he could find a solution for that or not. Over the next two hours, it was all about his reading out the notes of each person and telling them what he could solve and what he could not. Of course, he could not close the main matter by the end of those two hours. 'But that transparent approach broke the deadlock, created huge trust among those employees and we finally solved the problem in the next couple of weeks. Most people took the transfer to other units of the Jewellery division and are still working there,' Raj smiles in relief.

The company had rationale on its side. It was also legally fine to close that unit. The government authorities had also agreed with us on that. The number of employees was not large enough to create any major trouble for the company. But we chose to do it in this manner because we believed that employees are not resources.

C.K. Venkataraman

It was 11 a.m. on Diwali in 2012. As is usual for me on every Diwali day, I had finished an early shower and had a traditional breakfast of idli, coconut chutney and gun powder with gingelly oil. I was fully relaxed and in a holiday mood as I lounged on the sofa and shot off a text to Tarun Mukherjee, the store manager of our South Extension store in New Delhi. 'Hi Tarun, how's the day looking? Customers have started coming in?' Tarun's reply came thirty minutes later and shook me up completely, making me feel really selfish and uncaring. 'Sorry, Venkat. I have become an area business manager [ABM] in Delhi now and, for the first time in twenty-one years, am spending Diwali at home. I'll speak to Shiv (the new store manager) and revert by noon.' Of course! I suddenly remembered now that Tarun had moved out of the store a couple of months back. But what hit me was that every one of those twenty-one years that he, and other retail staff, had missed being with their families on Diwali day, I was blissfully enjoying Diwali at home with my family and enjoying the fruits of their sacrifice. That reply felt like a slap on my face. I apologized profusely to Tarun, asked him not to bother and that I would reach out to Shiv myself. This incident seared my soul and left an abiding desire to try and help the store staff as much as I could.

Shanthi, my executive assistant for many years, helped create a programme called 'Heart-to-Heart'. Cute, yellow, postcard-sized cards were distributed to field managers. On every one of my store visits, the ABM would get these cards filled, each with one staff member's name and their achievements. The most significant part of my visit would be the meeting with the store staff. The ABM would read out the descriptions (sometimes it would be some poetry as well) on each card and get the other members of the team to guess the name of that person. The mix of serious, funny and teasing descriptions would sometimes get the staff guessing wrong names, but mostly they would guess right, thus, generating much mirth. The person would then collect the card from me along with a chocolate and get a photo taken. In this event, I would also make it a point to include all the security guards, the housekeeping folks, the valet and any other person who supports the sales staff. If none of us from the store smiles at the security guards, if none of us appreciates what they do, then how can we expect them to welcome every customer with a smile, is the message that would get across.

How much do leaders think about the well-being of the 'troops'? How much do they think about the little gestures that can make them feel cared for?

Rajnarayan and I were on a stage at Titan's HR planning meet in 2017. Raj asked me what I would like the HR department to create afresh. I told him that, sometime in future, I would like many processes of Titan Company to be transferred to our franchisee ecosystem as well, for everyone's benefit. This conversation gave birth to the Business Associate Engagement (BAE) team within the HR function. The BAE function would end up creating multiple interventions. The five-essentials programme for the retail store staff of our franchisees (more than 15,000 of them): treating them with fairness and dignity through the issuance of proper appointment letters, giving them an ID badge, crediting of salaries by the third of each month, enrolling them into PF and ESI, setting up insurance for them; creating the Brand Ambassador Celebration Day where all the staff dress in whatever they want to, let their hair down, have fun, go out for dinner as a team; creating a platform for sharing the best people practices of benchmark franchisee partners for wide dissemination.

Swadesh Behera took over from Rajnarayan, who retired in June 2021. I took this opportunity to change the name of the HR function to People Function and the CHRO to CPO, chief people officer, which had been Bhaskar's intent and practice for a long time.

Titan had always been a People company. This value shone well during Covid when Titan showed its *unconditional Positive regard for People*. The People, in turn, took matters into their own hands and overcame all the challenges that the pandemic had put in front of the company, delivering great results that surprised everyone, including them.

During the pandemic, I had thought about this subject a whole lot and ended up creating an expression for our annual report. *Being Good is good for business*. It was something that I truly believed in.

Of course, there are other dimensions relating to employees that are equally crucial for sustained success: Organization Structure, People Capability, Performance Obsession, Rewards and Recognition. But perhaps much exists in management literature about these subjects, including how to do these well. This chapter was about an uncommon angle about People management, *of treating employees as People, and not as resources*. Titan and Tanishq believe in that principle and have practised it effectively for more than thirty-five years.

5

Leadership

How much time do leaders spend on the ground, particularly in the front? How infallible do they consider themselves? How open are they to criticism from all around? How much do they put themselves in the firing line?

It was sometime in 2009. 'Agartala? What are you doing in Agartala, man?' asked a curious friend of mine. Implicit in that tone was the view that the CEO's time is best spent in the metropolises of the world, hobnobbing with bankers and consulting company partners or in power breakfasts and golfing breaks with other CEOs and certainly with senior colleagues in HQ board rooms on matters of strategy. *What the hell are you doing in Agartala?* My answer has always been: spending all possible time with frontline employees at Tanishq has sharpened our strategy development and execution and generated the highest levels of motivation and morale among the 'troops'.

But does the CEO have to travel to Agartala for this – one could argue. Can't the organization create processes that bring all key issues to the HQ, where it gets adequate hearing? It's very much possible, of course, but I believe that such a process intrinsically favours the HQ and is loaded against the trenches.

Most decisions in business are about optimizing stakeholder interests.

If I give in to the request for a price drop, what will happen to profits? (Customer versus Company.) If I make the store processes simpler, am I risking lower compliance? (Employee versus Company.) When any optimization discussion happens in HQ, most of the decisions favour the company or shareholders, because of multiple factors at work. The voice from the trenches is often the most junior around the table and does not get as loud as it should be. The overall power distribution around the table is so lopsided in favour of the HQ that the field folks mostly don't stand a chance. The formality of the environment impedes frankness. But when you shift the location to Agartala, many things change. The voice from the trenches is direct to the CEO (the entire chain of command does not travel with the

CEO) and is buttressed by many other voices from the stores and franchisee partners. The store environment is more welcoming of feedback than the 'stiffness' of an HQ boardroom. Additionally, informal dinner situations on such travels help in strengthening the assertiveness of the trenches and the receptivity of the HQ.

It's this strong belief that creates wheels under my legs. For nearly fifteen years I have travelled, travelled and travelled. From Mumbai and Delhi to Jamnagar and Hisar and every other town in between, across west, north, east and south. Travels become my raison d'être, my source of inspiration and energy. It helps that the number of Tanishq stores is only in the hundreds and I am able to spend good quality time in every store. Appreciating the nuances, shaken and jolted by the emotions, all the time building more and more empathy for the troops. The battle analogy does not go all the way in what we are doing (everything that we do in Tanishq is about love, not war), but the analogy does help in bringing alive the aspect of troops and trenches and the HQ's responsibility in that context.

Two key factors enabled me to be on the road so much. One, for more than a decade I was blessed to have, among Sandeep Kulhalli, Revathi Kant and Sanjay Ranawade, three leaders who were totally on top of their domains and executed everything efficiently and in style. So, once we had agreed on the goals and the broad directions towards them (we have five-year strategy roadmaps), I was not really required in the HQ. I could travel as much as I wanted. Two, my management style as well philosophy made me delegate work entirely and the need to catch up with my deputies and their teams was just once a month. I used to share in large company forums that if I did not travel that much, I would have no work. People used to think that I was clever with my words, but, no, it was the truth.

The Chennai weather was balmy on that February morning in 2006. Latha Padmanabhan, at that time our area manager for Tamil Nadu, and Yashwant Kumar, our regional manager for South, and I were standing on the pavement outside the Tanishq Cathedral Road store (the first store of Tanishq set up in 1996) and staring at a large store of a competitor across the road. Some five or six customers had moved in and out of the store in the ten minutes that we were outside. I was just a year into Tanishq, with some of the rookie naivete still sticking to me. Latha was a decade-long veteran and Yashwant somewhere in between. The subject of discussion was the making charges of the Tanishq gold jewellery, perceived by all customers to be way too high, resulting in many people choosing not to buy. 'Venkat, if you add up the wastage that the Tamil Nadu jewellers charge in addition to the making charges that they also charge, we are not at all that badly off. But because we only have making charges, we come across as way too expensive,' Latha explains. I was still naïve enough to ask, 'But why can't we also break it up like that?' Latha and Yashwant gaped at me, wondering, *doesn't this guy know we are a brand? And a brand does not do things like that?* But their own desire for that solution pulled us into a detailed conversation on that subject. I went back to Bengaluru and initiated a change in our pricing strategy for Chennai in March (Tamil Nadu and the rest of South followed soon). Suddenly, our making charges were close to the competitors (and so was our 'wastage' which was a new term in our life then) and it was a whole new beginning in Chennai, Tamil Nadu and the South. Store conversions jumped and everyone was quite happy. Nothing had changed, yet *everything* had!

Multiple things favoured the voice of the trenches on this Chennai pavement that the Bengaluru boardroom would have discouraged. Feisty though that Latha was, the proximity to the CEO and the informal setting of the roadside emboldened her to speak with a certain frustration about the problem and shook me into giving it the importance it deserved. The fact that we were staring at a more popular competitor store added power to her argument. The absence of other HQ people around us, with possibly valid HQ counterpoints, made it easier for me to see her POV. That's the value of the CEO and other leaders being there with the frontline, as often as you can.

'Mr Venkat, your brand is much, much bigger than X (another up and coming national brand). You must be buying many times the gold that X is buying, and your cost should be lower than X's. How come your gold rate is higher than X's? I can understand Tanishq charging more for its design and quality, but why a higher gold rate?' This uncomfortable question was posed to me by a customer, in the middle of a customer meet I was holding in Amritsar sometime in 2010, as part of a customer-engagement programme we began in 2007.

Another big advantage of the travel is the opportunity to put yourself on the spot in front of customers. As the CEO, I really have nowhere to hide. If I can answer convincingly, then we can build a rationale for the whole organization. If I stutter and sputter, maybe that policy or that process needs change. In this Amritsar instance, my considered answer about the various parts of the Tanishq price (including the premium on the gold rate) and the various parts of the Tanishq value mollified the customer and built the foundation for the organizational belief in the justification for the gold rate.

How often do leaders meet customers themselves? Many customer-centric organizations would have systematic processes for understanding the needs and expectations of customers, of course, but *to listen directly to the voices of many customers* is priceless. The customer is never quite fazed by the fact that you are the CEO. They do not pull any punches! And when there are many customers that you are meeting together, you can be rest assured that nothing will be held back, and you will get the unvarnished truth. How valuable is that!

'Raji was flabbergasted, Venkat,' chuckled Amit Jalan, a Tanishq franchisee partner in West Bengal. I was meeting him in Kolkata at a regional franchisee conference, sometime in 2017. He was referring to my trip to his Tanishq store in Asansol six months earlier, where Rajeshwari Srinivasan (Raji), our then business head for the East Region, was not able to accompany me. Amit's laughter continued. 'A few hours after you left Asansol, Raji calls me to check on what all happened on your visit to the store.' What had happened was that the two field managers who had accompanied me and I had gone to Amit's (and his son Kunal's) store around 8 a.m. The women staff did a Rabindra-Sangeet dance performance in our honour, which we really loved. Then Sandeep Sarkar, another member of the staff and an exceptional singer, sang many wonderful songs. A mike and amp had been set up for this. As is my wont, and shameless that I was, I had also joined Sandeep on some of the songs. We all had a great time and then we left for Midnapore around 11 a.m. When Amit told Raji about all this, 'She asks me, what about the store metrics? Walk-in and conversion? GHS enrollment? Competition? Stock turn figures? Didn't Venkat ask questions around all those? I reply, no, there was only song and dance!' Amit was chortling as he concludes.

So, what is the actual role of the generals when they visit the trenches? There are multiple people in the chain of command who keep going to the front to discuss the tactics of war. Do the generals also need to that? Or is the army much better off when the generals do things that make the troops feel energized, confident, positive and inspired?

The most magical aspect of the last twenty years of my life has been the opportunity to be in these trenches frequently. The passion, energy, enthusiasm and commitment of the store staff, the franchisees, the field operations teams, the vendor partners and the *karigar*s have been a source of limitless energy, everlasting joy and absolute faith for me. Making me a much, much better person than who I was in 2004 before I entered the world of Tanishq.

It is all those people that I will sorely miss, not the title, not the power, not the trappings, when I hang up my boots on 31 December 2025.

In Conclusion

As I look back over the last twenty-seven years of Tanishq, what comes to mind is less the success of Tanishq, and more its lasting impact on the customer and the industry.

More and more customers today sleep totally in peace on account of the Karatmeter revolution that Tanishq started in 1997. Members of the Tanishq team have actively participated in the government's efforts to bring in hallmarking. Substantial work done on the diamond side, including industry-leading investments around diamond pipeline integrity (for ensuring ethically sourced natural diamonds, not mixed with any simulants) have added to that promise.

Industry-leading, transparent practices like charging the gold rate only on the net weight of gold in gem-set products; declaration of the weight of enamel for handcrafted jewellery; making sure that the weight and quality of diamonds in every piece is what is declared in the invoice: not only have these created the competitive edge for Tanishq, but these are also becoming more of the industry norm.

Reimagining the category from a 'store of value' to an 'object of desire', a 'lifestyle accessory' and a 'brand' through multiple transformational programmes: deep-design stories behind exquisite jewellery pieces; communication campaigns that evoked a more progressive world; democratization of diamonds, greater pull towards *kundan* and *polki* jewellery, conversion of the making charges as a percentage of the price of gold.

Preserving exquisite craft like *kundan* through movies like *Paheli* and *Jodhaa Akbar*, and breathing life into it. Fusing techniques like Cuttack filigree, *chandak* layering, dye work and Bikaneri *minakari* (enamelling) in a single piece, starting back in 2007, and showing the industry a way to impress even more customers and make profits while doing so.

Pioneering category management practices around store assortment and inventory levels as well as managing individual store profitability, all to deliver exceptional operational efficiencies, methods that more and more jewellery retail chains and progressive independents are starting to follow.

Establishing franchising at scale and reaching the deepest parts of India in the 2000s itself, showing the way for many others, paving the way for the formalization of the industry with speed and bringing quality to customers in the smallest of towns.

Bringing dignity to the artisan, giving respect and self-esteem to the tens of thousands of *karigar*s through its exemplary manufacturing transformation programmes like Unnati, Mr Perfect and 4-P and influencing the industry to follow suit.

The impact has been deep, wide and long-lasting. The industry will never be the same again.

C.K. Venkataraman
May 2024

Notes

1 Adrija Roychowdhury, 'The Kohinoor 'Curse' and Other Unknown Stories About the British Crown Jewel', *The Indian Express*, 16 February 2023, https://indianexpress.com/article/research/a-cursed-stone-or-mountain-of-darkness-why-the-kohinoor-never-really-impressed-the-british-or-their-monarchs-8162306/.

2 For a fascinating and comprehensive story of the entire Titan Company, please read *TITAN: Inside India's Most Successful Consumer Brand* by Vinay Kamath (Hachette India, 2018).

3 'Titan Watches Limited: Sixth Annual Report – 1989–90', https://www.titancompany.in/sites/default/files/2023-08/Annual%20Report%201989%20-%201990.pdf.

4 From Vinay Kamath's *Titan: Inside India's Most Successful Consumer Brand*

Notes

5 'Titan Industries Limited: Annual Report – 1996–97', https://www.titancompany.in/sites/default/files/2023-08/Annual%20Report%201996%20-%201997.pdf.

6 Making charges are what customers pay on top of the price of gold in a jewellery piece, and what they lose when they exchange that piece later as they get only the value of the gold in that piece at the time of exchange. Because of this they prefer to pay the lowest-making charges.

7 Thomas Edward Lawrence, *Seven Pillars of Wisdom*, Wordsworth Editions, 1997.

8 'Titan Industries: 20th Annual Report – 2003–2004', https://www.titancompany.in/sites/default/files/2023-08/Annual%20Report%202003%20-%202004.pdf.

9 'Titan Industries: 21st Annual Report – 2004–2005', https://www.titancompany.in/sites/default/files/2023-08/Annual%20Report%202004%20-%202005.pdf.

10 'Titan Industries: 32nd Annual Report – 2015–16', https://www.titancompany.in/sites/default/files/2023-08/Titan_AR_16.pdf.

Acknowledgements

The idea for this book was Chiki Sarkar's. Chiki was joined by Devangshu Datta in the critiquing of the writing, and both helped in shaping the actual structure of the book and the narrative. Thank you, Chiki and Devangshu. Thank you Team Juggernaut for all the support.

My thanks to Vinay Kamath, from whose book on Titan I borrowed a few facts and observations.

The Tanishq journey will forever remain the most fulfilling of my career, mostly because it made me a much better person.

Before I started writing, I talked to dozens of individuals who had participated in this beautiful journey that began in 1993. I had also been there for a good part of those years, and all those conversations made for some vivid memories coming alive. But the early part of the journey was not known to me, and it was a fascinating discovery.

Acknowledgements

The experiences were inspiring, powerful, moving, funny and helped build not just the story but its meaning as well.

My heartfelt thanks to everyone who took time to talk about their own part in this journey with passion, emotion, candour, nostalgia and pride.

However, for various reasons, not everyone's experiences found their way into the book. My apologies to those people. Also, the lessons drawn from the experiences are solely my conclusions and if they do not meet your expectations, the fault is entirely mine!

I would like to thank all of the following people:

Former Titan directors:

Ishaat Hussain, Ireena Vittal

Former/Current Titan executives:

Anil Manchanda, Sumant Sood, Kaladhar Mallem, Kalpana Kar;

David Saldanha, Meera Harish, Latha Padmanabhan;

Harish Bhat, V. Govind Raj, A. Palanikumar, S. Rajarathnam, Y.L. Saroja, Elizabeth Mathan, Antony Motha, Bharat Jhaveri, Aanchal Jain, Bhuwan Gaurav, Balaji Natarajan, A. Shivaram;

Acknowledgements

Sandeep Kulhalli, Saumen Bhaumik, Sunil Raj, Deepika Tewari, Rajan Amba, H. Ananthanarayanan, Niraj Bhakare, Anirban Banerjee, Munish Chawla, M. Alagappan, Bidyut Nath, Chitti Babu, Gaurav Midha, Sirish Chandrasekhar, Alpana Parida;

Revathi Kant, Anjali Sikka, Sangeeta Dewan, Queeta Rawat, V. Saravanan, Beate Steinfeld, M. Arivazhagan;

L.R. Natrajan, Sanjay Ranawade, P. Radhamanalan, P. Sukumaran, Anikesh Nandy, B. Manimaran, Biren Jhaveri;

S. Subramaniam, R. Rajnarayan, C. Ramachandran, B. Gopalarethinam, S. Keerthivasan, Dominic, C.H. Murali;

Ajoy Chawla, Kuruvilla Markose, Arun Narayan, R. Sharad, Vijay Govindarajan, Vijesh Rajan, Ranjani Krishnaswamy.

Titan Company franchisee/vendor partners/partner employees

Harinder Madaan, Jatin Parekh, Manoj Parsrampuria, Jogu Prasad, Ajeet Arenja; Gopi Panchal; Pawan Sharma; Vishal Saraogi;

Kamlesh and Rajesh Vyas, Sanjay Dugar, Sanjiv Kejriwal, Colin Shah, Sanjay Jaiswal, Kapil Soni, Anthony Thottan.

Acknowledgements

Formerly with Lintas/Lowe Lintas

R. Balki, Joe George, Rajesh Ramaswamy, Sudhir Rajasekharan, Deepa Geethakrishnan, Sharon Nayak; Josy Paul.

Others

Santosh Desai

My specific thanks to Sunil Raj, with whom I have had so many shared experiences in the Tanishq journey and who took so much trouble to read two versions of the draft and suggest some improvements as well as some synthesis, and to Dinesh Shetty for also going through the two versions and suggesting some modifications.

My final thanks to Jacob Kurian and Bhaskar Bhat, the two heroes of the story – the first for infusing so much life and energy into Tanishq just when it was needed, and the second for building Titan Company into the institution it is today.

My wife and daughters were with me all the way, wanting me to succeed in this dream. Padma, my younger daughter, influenced me in finding my own voice in the story. Thank you, my three lovely women!

C.K. Venkataraman